ERASMUS

and

OUR STRUGGLE FOR PEACE

ERASMUS *and*

Our Struggle for Peace

Erasmus: Herald of a United World

by JOSÉ CHAPIRO

●

Peace Protests!

by ERASMUS OF ROTTERDAM

*Translated, with an Introduction and Notes,
by José Chapiro*

Boston ∘ THE BEACON PRESS ∘ *1950*

THIS BOOK ON PEACE AND A UNITED WORLD

IS DEDICATED

TO THE

UNITED NATIONS

EMBODIMENT OF THE IDEALS OF ERASMUS

AND

SOURCE OF THE HIGHEST HOPES OF OUR TIMES

Contents

Erasmus has published volumes more full of wisdom than any which Europe has seen for ages.

SIR (SAINT) THOMAS MORE (1478-1535)

These great evils which men inflict on one another because of divergent tendencies, because of passions, opinions, and creeds, all spring from a *lack*, for they all result from ignorance — that is, lack of knowledge. Just as the blind man, because of the lack of sight, constantly bumps himself, hurts himself and even hurts others where there is no one to guide him, so hostile parties of men, each according to the degree of their ignorance, inflict, on themselves and on others, evils which weigh heavily on the individuals of the human race. If they possessed knowledge, which is to human form what the visual faculty is to the eye, they would be prevented from doing any harm to themselves and to others; for the knowledge of the truth ends intolerance and hatred, and prevents men from inflicting reciprocal evil.

MOSES MAIMONIDES (b. in Cordoba, Spain, 1135; d. in Cairo, Egypt, 1204) in *The Guide for the Perplexed* (*Dalalat Hairim*)

You are meeting this year under the dark clouds of a threat of war. But you should be reassured in your decision to go along increasing your knowledge of the world, because *lack* of such knowledge is the basis of trouble in the world today.

DWIGHT D. EISENHOWER, president of Columbia University, speaking at the opening exercises of the University's fifty-first summer session, on July 10, 1950

We will have these great United States of Europe which will crown the old world as the United States of America crown the new. We will have the spirit of conquest transfigured into the spirit of discovery. . . . We will have a country without a frontier, a budget without parasitism, commerce without custom houses, travel without barriers, education without stultification, youth without military barracks, courage without battle, justice without the scaffold, life without murder, . . . the plow without the sword, the word without the gag, conscience without the yoke, truth without dogma, God without the priest, Heaven without Hell, love without hate.

VICTOR HUGO, in his message of September 20, 1872, to the International Congress of Peace at Lugano (Switzerland)

To the Reader

THIS BOOK IS ADDRESSED to the general reader. Although the result of long years of study and research, it is intended not exclusively for scholars and specialists, as are most of the publications about Erasmus. In writing *Erasmus: Herald of a United World* and in translating *Peace Protests!* from the Latin, my purpose was to popularize the most fascinating but least known aspect of Erasmus' personality: the uncommonly courageous pacifist, many centuries ahead of the time in which he lived; his relentless struggle for a world of united nations; his constructive ideas on peace, which clarify our own while amplifying them.

Therefore, and in order to avoid anything susceptible of lessening the interest of the reader or of making the reading of the book less comfortable, I have omitted footnotes completely and avoided references insofar as they are not indispensable for the grasp of the character and the better understanding of the pacifist ideas of Erasmus. Thus *Peace Protests!* is followed by some notes which may widen the horizon on Erasmus, but my own text is not. Nevertheless, the scholar acquainted with the rich and steadily growing literature about the most distinguished humanist of the Renaissance will notice that, in writing my book, I have covered, in half a dozen languages, the most authoritative sources and works — from the oldest to the most recent — about the author of *Peace Protests!*

The time and toil I have spent in the translation of this

great peace manifesto and in the research for my own text would be largely compensated if, without being disapproved by scholars, I should have succeeded in interesting the general reader.

In telling the story of Erasmus' struggle for peace, I have had to deal in this book on peace not only with his political attacks against warlike kings and other warmongers but also — reluctantly, I confess — with some of his theological controversies with Rome and with Luther. True, I have not enlarged on his criticisms of certain distinctive features of the creeds mentioned. I have spoken only generally of the latter, insofar as the two opposed religious currents of the time interfered with Erasmus' general conception of peace. Erasmus himself, with his uncompromising tolerance and with his plea for the right of everyone to err in his own way, would probably not have dedicated so much space to such questions if he had not been forced to do so by the violence of his opponents. For specific tenets and practices in creeds did not mean much to Erasmus, who considered them as obscuring and corrupting true religion rather than adding something valuable to it.

Moreover, utterances in this category varied according to the foe whom Erasmus was addressing. Out of love for peace and his desire to reconcile the disputing parties so as to accomplish a Reformation on a universal scale, and thus to realize his dream of a truly universal religion, he defended against Luther certain features peculiar to the Catholic creed, in spite of his own life-long attacks against the Church of Rome; and at the same time, while accusing Luther of having introduced a new tyrannical dogmatism in addition to that already existing, he defended the purity of the life and many of the arguments of the German reformer when the latter was calumniated, excommunicated, persecuted and

branded by Rome. That is why it is so easy — and consequently cheap — for partisan critics to find in the theological
considerations of Erasmus certain contradictions, if the in-
alterable spirit in which they were uttered is neglected. It is
this very spirit which makes Erasmus the originator of most
of the great generous movements in modern times.

Having been the target of both opposing religious currents
of his age, he continued to be so in the books of his partisan
biographers and interpreters, Lutheran as well as Catholic,
through the centuries; and he still is. I have abstained from
refuting them thoroughly and from discussing the religious
beliefs of Erasmus in any other way than in connection with
his ideals of peace. For to Erasmus, material or political
peace, nationally and internationally, was inconceivable
without spiritual peace, and all of them were unthinkable
without being intimately associated with democratic freedom.
His universality was truly all-embracing.

This is to say that Erasmus was not an ideologist in the
sense in which we conceive this word today. He belonged to
no party and took the good wherever, and in whatever
amount, he could find it. This point is worthy of emphasis in
introducing the ideas of the author of *Peace Protests!* I
quote in my book the definition Erasmus gave of a free man.
He said that free men guide and are willing to be guided,
whereas slaves and asses are driven, and tyrants drive. The
school of thought of Erasmus was that of a free man. His
philosophy of life in its general and higher sense is thus
based on the free will and the free consent of the individual.
This philosophy, as practiced and taught by Erasmus, may
constantly be, and actually is, enriched by contributions of
free thinking citizens; its sources are thus continuously controlled, tested, and renewed by general consent. That is
ideal democracy. Whereas ideology, in its modern sense, is
a school of thought which, even if originally freely accepted,
forces its adherents to be dominated and driven by an im-

posed idea instead of dominating and mastering that idea themselves, in the light of daily experiences and widening knowledge. One is flexible, the other static; one is adjustable, the other rigid; the sources of one are constantly enriched, the spring of the other fatally doomed to dry out.

I am mentioning the fact of ideologies in connection with the pacifism of Erasmus because peace is becoming the slogan of ideologies. Nay, peace is becoming an ideology in itself! And here lies its greatest danger. As long as love of peace was ridiculed and despised or ignored just as much as the ideals of perfect cosmopolitanism and democracy, its foes were visible even to the poorest sight. But the ideologists are now using and abusing this magic word in a sense which makes it its own foe — that is, contrary to itself. In the name of peace they invite to hatred, hatred against all those who disagree with them in whatever field it may be, even in matters of art. Whereas, as Erasmus pointed out, peace is a composite resulting from mutual enrichment through mutual concessions; a whole, not a part; the sum of the good will of all, not a surrender to the unyielding will of one, in addition driven by hatred. Unhappily, the ideological distortion of the meaning of peace produces the most disastrous effects, and — surprisingly enough — in both directions. We must take care that *who hates whom* should not become everywhere, little by little, the determining factor in the definition of the nature of peace we strive for. At least not in the countries where free thinking is the great privilege of their citizens.

Peace as an ally of hatred is a monstrous aberration. This is not the peace of Erasmus and it is not peace at all. What it meant to him and what peace can only be and how we shall learn it — "the art of peace" — Erasmus explained in various of his works which I summarize in my study on *Erasmus: Herald of a United World*. And of these *Peace Protests!* is the most powerful expression.

The texts quoted throughout this book, whether from Erasmus or from other authors, have all, except some passages from Scriptures, been newly translated by myself from the various languages—Arabic, French, German, Italian, Latin —in which they were originally written. My sources for quotations from Erasmus were, without exception, the two standard editions of his works and letters in the original Latin: *Desiderii Erasmi Roterodami Opera Omnia,* Lugduni Batavorum [Leyden, Holland], 1703-1706, Editio Clericus [LeClerc], 10 vols.; and the complete edition of his letters: *Opus Epistolarum Des. Erasmi Roterodami,* by P. S. Allen and Mrs. H. M. Allen, Oxford 1906-1947, 11 vols.

For the Biblical quotations on which, in *Peace Protests!,* Erasmus rests his arguments, I have borrowed the English text from the King James Version, indicating each time the exact source. However, Erasmus often amplified these quotations, making a direct translation necessary.

JOSÉ CHAPIRO

Petersham, Massachusetts
1950

PART ONE

ERASMUS: HERALD OF A UNITED WORLD
by José Chapiro

1.

Why Erasmus?

ERASMUS, who during his lifetime was the most famous and most widely read author in Europe, wrote in Latin. In the course of the centuries, this language, which made his works accessible to the cultivated world of the Renaissance and the Reformation, has become the principal obstacle to their diffusion. In his ardent faith in the progress and the triumphant march of humanity toward its enlightened liberation and its moral elevation, Erasmus refused to write in a modern tongue, not only as a matter of taste and idealism but, with an eye on the future, for what he believed to be *practical* reasons.

In his struggle for political as well as spiritual peace, Erasmus dreamed of a religion which, freed from dogmas that divided men and made them intolerant to the point of cruelty, would unite them all in the same ardent faith. And he dreamed of a world community in which all nations would merge, as the rivers mingle with the sea. Only universality in spiritual and political domains, he believed, offered the infallible condition for ending war and hatred, as peace was the most perfect means of raising men to a position worthy of their name. Each nation being the sum of the individuals who composed it, the supernational state would be worth only as much as the nations that were merged in it. The value of each nation, however, is determined exclusively by the degree of education of its people. Thus, a world diffusion of moral, religious, and general education became the principal object of his thought.

Erasmus remains one of the greatest educators of humanity. Seeking for practical methods for its inculcation, he saw in the Humanism of the Renaissance not only the magical instrument that would spread learning throughout the world but the most effective method of education. For this purpose a universal language — a vehicle of comprehension among individuals, nations, and races — was indispensable. To set an example, he himself spoke only Latin and wrote only in that language, convinced that the tongue which for centuries had been that of scholars and of the Church would finally impose itself on all men of all times. In it and through it, humanity would some day be united.

In this concept, the man who was so far-seeing and clear-sighted in the darkness of his own time appears to have been mistaken. Otherwise, some part at least of his works would today be at the very core of international discussion — particularly his little work whose Latin title is *Querela Pacis,* which literally means *The Complaint of Peace,* and which, adapting it to the idiom of our own time, I have translated as *Peace Protests!*

Querela Pacis, a masterpiece in itself, merits our attention as the masterpiece of pacifist literature. But how is this attention to be attracted? Our century — after two world wars, with their incalculable millions of dead and wounded, the unspeakable horrors which accompanied them, the gas chambers, massacres of innocents, tortures, hunger, and the rest — our century, I say, is too accustomed to grief to be easily moved by the complaints of peace pleading its own cause, even though the cause is our own. We live in an age where the radio and unbridled propaganda demand our attention, deafening us to submerged voices which are only plaintive, unless we have the strength constantly to struggle against the current. Not that we have become less sensitive or less charitable than the generations before us — neither charity nor compassion has ever been manifested on a greater scale than in the present generation. But surrounded by noise, we do not notice complaints until the victim begins to break windows, to bawl in the streets, to turn his quiet complaint into a thundering accusation, into a roar of indignant protest.

This protest cannot shout too loud when it comes to denouncing the crime that is being perpetrated, in spite of our horror of war — whether because we are blinded by habit, or by the pernicious propaganda against which Erasmus warned us so long ago, or by our apathy, or even by our conscious fatalism which amounts to complicity. That is why, translating both meaning and tone in terms of present-day receptivity and current events, I chose the title of *Peace Protests!*

Later on, I will explain the character of my translation. Meanwhile, I would like to make clear that I have not undertaken this translation out of mere curiosity or that kind of veneration displayed by visitors at museums before masterpieces and the great masters of the past, but because, having hated war and labored for peace all my life, I see in the 450-year-old *Peace Protests!* a striking expression of our own aspirations and our own indignation; and because, in the ideological and spiritual confusion which characterizes our epoch, this masterpiece supplies the fundamental work on peace which our generation has not yet been able to produce, in spite of the many books which continually appear on the subject. In translating *Peace Protests!*, therefore, I felt that I was filling a void and that Erasmus, speaking through a modern tongue, might help to discredit war as well as hasten the hour of peace among all men.

It was not only in *Peace Protests!* that Erasmus spoke of this subject. With clarity and surprising modernism, these pathetic accents of peace abused and driven out everywhere are heard in some of his other works which, paradoxically, have remained both famous and unread, just as their author, one of the noblest and most glorious spirits of history, is one of the most misknown. Thus his position and his political ideas, as they emerge from his life and other works besides *Peace Protests!*, are worth a moment's consideration before we pass on to the reading of this manifesto on peace, which was their culmination as well as their most perfect expression.

2.

The Modernism of Erasmus

THE CASE OF ERASMUS OF ROTTERDAM — monk, priest, theologian, traveler, philosopher, poet, writer, polemicist, pacifist — is an extraordinary one. It is rare to encounter a person of average culture who is not familiar with his name, but it is exceptional to find those who know more of him than that he was a great humanist. If one insists on more definite information, one will be told that he lived during the Renaissance and that, as a contemporary of Luther and Zwingli, he contributed to the Reformation of the Church.

There is little in this to justify the lively memory we keep of his name. Besides, so far as the Reformation is concerned, Erasmus neither established a sect nor formulated a new creed with which his name is associated, as is the case of a Luther or a Calvin or even lesser reformers. Indeed, the *active* role played by a Melanchthon infinitely surpasses that of Erasmus. And yet everyone knows the name of the latter, while few know that of Luther's first lieutenant. Moreover, opinions on his role in the triumph of the Reformation are not only divided, but diametrically opposed, according to the camp expressing them. The Catholics who, after his death, put many of his works on the Index, accuse him of having shaken the Church of Rome to its foundations and of being the real father of Lutheranism and the revolt against Rome in general. Luther, on the other hand, accused him at times of papistry, at times of atheism; and the Lutherans point out the fact that he never renounced his Catholic faith.

7

Obviously, such an explanation of the popularity of the name of Erasmus does not take us far.

As for his works, only rarely do we find people who have read more than *Praise of Folly* or his *Colloquies*. These sparkling satires are undoubtedly masterpieces, but literary history possesses others on which the dust of centuries accumulates so thickly that only a scattering of scholars venture to encumber their memories with the dusty names. Perhaps it is as well that this should be so. Perhaps one would do some of these venerable names a disservice by attempting to dust them off or arouse them from the depth of the parchment caves where they sleep their profound sleep in a corner of our libraries.

No, the *Colloquies* and *Praise of Folly* could hardly rescue Erasmus from the forgetfulness which weighs pitilessly on so many other illustrious names. His glory lies elsewhere. His enduring fame is nourished by another spring than that of traditional respect for a great name of the past. Erasmus is neither a mummy nor a relic. On the contrary, his work, or rather his thought, constitutes one of those reservoirs of ideas to which our century — the century of "One World," as the late Wendell Willkie called it — may soon appeal, as the eighteenth century, the century of Jean-Jacques Rousseau's *Social Contract*, the Rights of Man, and the antimonarchist revolutions, appealed to it for other reasons.

The case of Erasmus is suggestive on more than one point. Why are we more familiar with certain men of the past than with others who were equally admired during their lifetime? Since — as far as we are not specialists — we read neither, what determines this choice in our memory? As anyone can verify from his own experience, it is neither the critics nor the historians nor our own judgment. Our choice is due to other factors. It is spontaneous, it belongs to the domain of irrational logic. As though guided by an unconscious presentiment of its future needs, the memory of

humanity retains names — one might say instinctively — as
reserves of moral energy. As in the case of Erasmus, we are
often ignorant even of the titles of their works, let alone
their ideas, although we apply them unconsciously in life.
Nonetheless, we feel that if one of these rare names were
allowed to fall into oblivion, our general and individual culture would suffer an irreparable impoverishment. Consequently, we celebrate their centenaries — while isolated, curi-
ous minds weigh once more their values, strip away the
parts that have become obsolete, free what is still alive, compare these ideas with those of their own century, and draw
up a new balance, thus aligning these re-evaluated values not
only with those of their contemporaries but with those of
future generations as well. Who knows whether our children
will not feel closer to them than we, closer even than those
who lived at the period in which these ideas were formulated,
as though the passing centuries narrowed rather than extended the time which separated them?

In the domain of ideas, there are areas in which to turn
back is to progress. Not that history, endlessly advancing,
permits real returns: yesterday can never become today. That
is so true that when one attempts to draw up a balance
sheet of his own generation, his conclusions are often out
of date by the time he arrives at them. Perhaps we must
conclude, like our own American reformer, William Ellery
Channing, that "the most eminent philosopher is of yesterday." And yet, undeniably, while advancing, we turn back
at certain periods to the past as though, in leaving it, we had
forgotten to bring with us something substantial. Does that
mean that from time to time humanity retraces the course
of history to repeat its stages?

Let us not deceive ourselves. Like all maxims of its kind,
"History repeats itself" is only half true, albeit we are constantly borrowing from the past. It is as though we were
always playing with the same ball. However — so says Pascal

— it is not so much the ball that distinguishes the players as the way they play. So it is with the eternal verities of the past. We turn back with new eyes and a new way of feeling, and thus, on each return, the same idea or the same work takes on an entirely different aspect from that which it had at the moment of its creation. We accept it not for what it was, but for what it is to us; we see it and interpret it differently from the contemporaries of the author or the artist, and we discover horizons which the latter perhaps never even suspected. To a certain extent, we probably understand it better than he himself understood it — whereas *he* would be incapable of understanding us. It is the eternal problem of fathers and sons: the latter draw their substance from the former, who endow them with physique, habits, ideas, tastes. But little by little, all is transformed and takes on so new an aspect that the children seem unrecognizable to the fathers.

So at certain periods in the evolution of humanity, the only way to advance is to turn back. This is true of art and this is true of moral ideas. The number of the latter is astonishingly limited. They seem many only because each generation decks them out with a freshness and originality which give them an air of being the most recent creation of contemporary genius. The same truth will vary, as though each generation supplied its own, and it will vary according to place as well as time. This phenomenon seems particularly striking when an idea is transplanted from one civilization to another.

How many admirable moral treatises have been composed in the past thirty or forty centuries, in how many languages and in how many latitudes! We no sooner evoke the titles in our memory than the greatest names arise before our dazzled minds — extraordinary geniuses whom we often call divine and who continue to enrich the human race. But when we reduce them to the simplest formula, do we find many new principles added to the eternal verities stated from Mount

Sinai or, fifteen centuries later, from the mountain top in Galilee? And are we sure that even those were as new in their time as they appeared to be? However primitive the Biblical patriarchs seem to us, these principles, under another form, were doubtless theirs too, while they themselves walked on the ruins of old civilizations from which they drew their moral sustenance.

To such fundamental ideas of our own times belong those on peace contained in *Peace Protests!* Moreover, even the form in which Erasmus clothed them retains all its suggestive power. It is much more of our age than it was of his own.

This *J'accuse!* by Peace rang out in 1517 against the monstrous abuses of the powerful, of the politicians, of the warmongers and of the spiritual leaders. For *Peace Protests!* was a defiance, a manifesto hurled in the face of those who controlled the physical as well as the moral and spiritual destinies of humanity. Nevertheless, its chief value does not lie in its specific criticisms, particularly in our days when there are almost no more kings, when the Church of Rome has lost its temporal power, and when those who sacrifice us to their own interests, follies, or narrow-mindedness are of far more modest origins.

The modernism and originality of the constructive ideas of *Peace Protests!* lie not least in the rallying cry that rang out across frontiers and centuries, calling upon the peoples to unite in one pan-human community for the establishment of perpetual peace. In *Peace Protests!,* more than in any of his other works, Erasmus soars to the height of a universal conscience. Perhaps today, at the end of nearly half a millennium, he might well be called upon to become a spokesman of our own aspirations for peace. In fact, no period was closer than our own to his ideas on peace, because the longing for "One World" was never so conscious or so general as today. No past generation had perhaps the means to carry them out so radically as our own.

3.

The Man

PEACE PROTESTS! was a logical climax toward which all the literary activities and all the spiritual and humanistic aspirations of Erasmus converged. So it is fitting, before we proceed to analyze his political and moral ideas — two adjectives which were one in his mind — to recall his antecedents; to indicate his intellectual and moral growth; to observe various stages of his literary career, so closely bound with that which marked his pacifist manifesto; to assess the leading traits of his character without which we would have only an incomplete idea of our author. For the man and the work constantly reflect each other, just as they complement each other.

The origins of Erasmus are obscure. There is not the slightest record of his birth or of his baptism. We are sure neither of his name nor of the date of his birth; and our author himself, instead of enlightening us, has only added to the confusion by his continual contradictions even in regard to the year in which he came into the world. We are therefore forced to content ourselves with conjectures and to conclude that he was probably born in Rotterdam in October, 1466, "on the Vigil of Simon and Jude," to quote Erasmus, and that he was the illegitimate son of a priest named Gerard and a woman named Margaret, who appears to have been the churchman's housekeeper.

At that time, it was quite common for nobles and princes to have one or several bastard children. Because of their fathers' powerful position, these children enjoyed brilliant

careers in society, in government, and — last but not least —
in the ecclesiastical hierarchy of the Church of Rome. Philip
of Burgundy, for instance — to whom Erasmus dedicated
Peace Protests! in the hope that he would use his enormous
political influence to contribute to the realization of lasting
peace — was both a bastard and a bishop, a position in which
he succeeded his older brother, who was also a bastard and
who ordained Erasmus as a priest.

On the other hand, illegitimate children of modest parents,
like Erasmus, found themselves from the beginning handicapped by virtually insurmountable obstacles. Their rights
were extremely limited, especially in countries which, like
Holland, formed part of the Holy Roman Empire. The German civil code imposed such drastic restraints on them that
they found advancement almost impossible. For example,
these unfortunate children could not make a free choice of
their profession; and if they did manage to make a fortune,
they could not dispose of it as they liked, for the benefit of
their heirs. But of all careers, that of the Church was the
hardest for them to enter, particularly for one who was the
son of a priest. For the latter, from the believer's point of
view, was because of his very title a *father;* consequently, all
sexual relations of a priest were regarded as incestuous, and
any child of his as a product of incest. Such a child could not
himself become a priest except by enrolling first in a monastic order and then, as a monk, being ordained in due
time. But even as a monk, he could not mount high in
the scale of the ecclesiastical hierarchy. If Erasmus succeeded
in surmounting all these obstacles, socially as well as in
the Church — which eagerly offered him bishoprics, posts
at the Vatican, and even the Cardinal's hat, without his ever
seeking them — he owed it to his genius alone.

Nevertheless, even at the peak of his fame, when the
most powerful men on earth paid court to him and were
proud to call him friend or even possess no more than a

letter from him, he never ceased to suffer from his unavowable antecedents. In their attacks, his enemies did not fail to make use of his handicap and even to add odious calumnies to the real facts. Think of Julius Caesar Scaliger who, in his pamphlets against Erasmus, went so far as to claim that his mother had been a common prostitute. A forceful polemicist who spent much of his life in violent attack and counter attack, Erasmus never refuted the calumnies regarding his birth, whether from dignity or because it was too painful for him to discuss publicly. We find no direct mention of it except in his brief autobiographical essay, entrusted to a friend and published about a century after his death, and in that moving letter which, when he was about fifty years old, he addressed to his friend, Pope Leo X. But even in this 10,000-word letter, which reads like a breathtaking novel, he pretended, lest it fall into the wrong hands, not to be making his own confession, but to be speaking of his "friend Florence" whose cause he was pleading, while he addressed the Pope as "Lambertus Grunnius, Apostolic Protonotary," a person that never existed.

In this letter, Erasmus undoubtedly told the truth, not only because of his natural honesty but because he was confessing to the Pope in the hope of being protected against his monastery, which, after his absence of nearly twenty-five years and many futile attempts to get him back, was still ordering him to return. But even in this moving confession, which breathes absolute sincerity, we find disturbing contradictions which the Pope did not fail to perceive and even to note in his confidential letter to Andrew Ammonius, the subcollector of Peter's Pence in England. To him Leo X wrote bluntly that he was certain Erasmus was the child of an illicit and even, he feared, damnable and incestuous union *(ex illicito et, ut timet, incesto damnatoque coitu genitus)*. However, to Erasmus the Pope pretended to believe all that he had stated about his birth, granting him the legitimate name of "Desiderius Erasmus, son of Rogerius" (which was no doubt the patronymic of his father), instead of "Erasmus, son of Margaret," and freeing him from all his outward obligations toward his monastic order, at the same time allowing him to dispense with certain religious duties that were required of all Catholics, and particularly of a monk and a priest. Erasmus carried this document with him until his death.

Probably these contradictory statements of Erasmus about his antecedents grew in part out of what his mother must have told him when he was a child, a pious tale which he would never admit to be untrue in spite of all the evidence against it; but chiefly they were a result of his early sufferings. At the time of the Renaissance, several of the greatest men — Leonardo da Vinci, for example — had similar antecedents, without appearing to suffer from them or to feel handicapped by them. But the case of Erasmus, son of a priest, appears in a totally different light. From his youngest years, he must have endured such frightful humiliations that they left scars on his soul which could never be effaced. Even at the peak of his fame his emotional wounds were not healed. His antecedents became an obsession from which he was unable to free himself. This sovereign intelligence, superior in lucidity, logical thinking, and sure judgment, this innate intellectual authority which was part of his genius, all his exceptional endowments became idiotically confused as soon as he began to write of his antecedents. In such moments, the man who had so keen a sense of the ridiculous and who towered so proudly above prejudice made himself ridiculous. This is a case of psychic pathology in which literary criticism yields to psychoanalysis.

Many of his biographers believe that he named himself Erasmus, and that he had been baptized with his father's name, Gerard or Gerhard. They supposed that this name, coming from the German or Dutch root *begehren* (to "desire

ardently"), was transformed by him into the adjective
"Erasmus" — *Erasmios* or rather *Herasmios* meaning "love"
in Greek. In my opinion this hypothesis is baseless. The
error probably comes from the belief that no one before him
had had this name. But among the twenty-five or thirty
thousand saints recorded by the Catholic Church, I have
found two of this name who lived before him, and the
humanist himself, in his *Praise of Folly,* refers to Saint
Erasmus. Nor do I believe that the priest Gerard would have
dared admit officially his paternity by baptizing his son with
his own name. In spite of the mores of that age and his
deep affection for his son, it would have been carrying his
defiance too far in the eyes of Rome and his own flock.
But, wanting nonetheless to call him, even in a hidden
way, by his own name, and knowing the meaning of the
word Erasmus, he must have baptized him thus. If his son,
a far greater scholar than he, had chosen the name, he would
have done it correctly: *Erasmius* or *Herasmius.* When he
became a famous Hellenist, the missing *i* and *h* must have
tortured his humanistic conscience every time he had to
sign his name. (In his youth, however, he called himself
Herasmus and was so called by his friends. Later he dropped
the *H,* surely because he had been baptized after Saint Erasmus. Monk and priest, he had to respect his baptismal name.)

Be that as it may, the meaning of this name must have
avenged him in his own eyes every time that, in the schools
of Gouda, Utrecht, 's-Hertogenbosch, or Deventer, and perhaps even at the monastery of Steyn, he was assailed as a
"bastard." But this name alone was not enough. Soon
he used it as a patronymic, preceding it with a Latin first
name, *Desiderius,* which means "the desired one" — as though
to underline the fact that he had been desired and welcomed
by his parents. Then he added to these two names the
adjective of his place of birth. In accordance with the
customs of old families, he thus reinforced his antecedents,

and his name finally became Desiderius Erasmus Rotero-
damus.

Besides its hidden, sentimental meaning, such a name
had still another significance. At the time of the Renaissance
it was good taste for a scholar to Latinize or Hellenize his
name, as though to give evidence of a rupture with the barbaric world. Thomas More called himself Morus. Schwarz-
erd, Luther's first lieutenant, called himself Melanchthon,
which is the Greek translation of his German name and
means "black earth." Erasmus' editor, Froben, Latinized
his name to Frobenius. And the same was true of many
of the scholars of that time. These were titles of nobility
with which the humanists of the Renaissance endowed themselves, in manifest contradistinction to the nobility of blood
for which their respect was no greater than for the mass of
the illiterate people. They appreciated but one kind of
knighthood —that which only knowledge and genius bestow.

While he was still a little boy, Erasmus lost his mother and
soon afterwards his father. Before his death, the priest
Gerard confided the education of his son, as well as all
his savings (which, with those of Margaret, were apparently
not negligible), to the care of guardians. These scoundrels
administered the heritage so well that by the time the orphan
reached the age of eighteen, and began to make plans for
the future, nothing remained. So, having already placed him
in a school managed by a monastery, they began to persuade
him to take orders. Erasmus was violently opposed to this
plan. But with the help of the monks who used wiles and
threats, tenderness and force — as Erasmus wrote to the Pope
— the guardians broke his will. A penniless bastard, he took
the vows.

Having become a monk against his will, he immediately
set to work to find means of leaving the monastery. For this

purpose he became a priest so that he could obtain dispensations to leave his order temporarily in order to carry out his other duties. Six years after having taken his second vows as an Augustine friar, he was ordained a priest in 1492 — curiously enough, almost simultaneously with the discovery of America by Christopher Columbus. Erasmus was then about twenty-six years old. Two years later, he succeeded in obtaining from his prior the first dispensation to occupy the post of Latin secretary to the Bishop of Cambrai. On its expiration he succeeded in having it renewed so that he could go to Paris to study at the Sorbonne for the degree of doctor of theology. Erasmus was about thirty when he arrived in the French capital.

Once he had left the monastery of Steyn, he did not return, except, for the last time, six or seven years later for a visit of a few hours to get his dispensation extended. From 1501 on he never set foot in it, although for nearly a quarter of a century he ran the risk of being brought back by force. Indeed, through an agreement with the Holy See, all Christian states were obligated to arrest fugitive or rebellious monks and return them to their respective monasteries.

Erasmus never forgave the monks. Every passing day made him more conscious of the crime that had been committed against him. "They made him wear the habit," he wrote in his letter to the Pope, relating the vicissitudes of his "friend Florence," "but they never got his consent. His oath, which was torn from him, was the kind one makes to a band of pirates." All his life he contested the validity of an oath made under such circumstances. Nevertheless, and in spite of having been allowed by the Pope to live privately and no longer to dress like a monk, he could never be freed from his oath. Erasmus died a monk — although by aptitude and aspiration, by taste and temperament, he was hardly made for the cloistered life.

When Erasmus was about forty-eight, Father Servatius, the

prior of the monastery of Steyn, undiscouraged by his previous refusals, made a new attempt to get Erasmus back to the cloister; thereupon the latter decided to divulge the whole matter to the Pope and sent the above-mentioned letter to "Grunnius." "You know," Erasmus wrote to the prior, "that I was *forced* by interested guardians to take orders. My physical constitution was too frail to endure your rule. I was devoted to literature. I knew that I might be happy and useful as a man of letters. But to break my vow was considered a crime and I tried to bear the yoke of my misery. My profession as a monk was a mistake."

This letter to the prior, who had known Erasmus since he entered his monastery, corroborates the one to "Grunnius" written two years later and establishes unquestionably the authenticity of his story about his monachal profession.

When he had gained enough liberty to do so, he began to take his revenge. He attacked all the orders so effectively that it took a long period of counter-reform for them to rehabilitate themselves. In several of his works, in thousands of his letters, some of which are famous, he missed no occasion to strike at the monks with his sarcasm and his wit, making all Europe — popes and cardinals included — shake at their expense with a Homeric laughter which might have made Olympian gods themselves envious.

Nor was Erasmus more tender with the clergy. From top to bottom of the ecclesiastical ladder, from the pope to the humblest priest, he stung them with his sarcasm and his criticism, marshaling all his gifts as theologian and writer, as psychologist and judge of men, as polemicist and incomparable strategist. He was, moreover, the wittiest man of the Renaissance. But it was not only by these great qualities as writer and thinker that he dominated his contemporaries. The man himself exerted the greatest attraction, by his personal charm, which opened hearts and palaces to him, by his gifts as a fascinating conversationalist, by his gentle manner, by his pure life, and not least by his genius for friendship.

4.

His Character

HIS ORIGINALITY SHONE OUT in everything he did and was. In this man whose naturalness was reflected so admirably in his style and his thought, his manners and his voice, everything was paradoxical. That is genius. And like a true genius, he overturned all the theories on the influence of environment and the times in which one lives.

Erasmus was born in Holland, in a foggy, nordic country. But in temperament, taste, and style, he was a thorough Latin — perhaps, to quote the French historian Michelet, the most Italianate writer of his epoch. He came into the world at a moment when European nations were becoming conscious of their geographical frontiers, when budding nationalism drove them to such exclusiveness that, starting with Luther, some even created national religions.

And yet there was never a man more naturally cosmopolitan or less nationalistic than Erasmus. Indeed, European cosmopolitanism in its *modern* sense might be said to date from Erasmus. At a time when Latin took refuge in theology, and national literatures were arising in various tongues, Erasmus deliberately brought the Latin tongue back to glorious life; for at least ten centuries no one had handled it with such perfection, and no one has ever done so again. He revived the Latin of the Augustan age, as a spoken tongue and in literature of every kind: his poetry, satire, dramatic dialogues, essays, criticism, political and theological polemics, translations of the Greek fathers and classics, and,

20

of course, his correspondence — all bear witness to his unexcelled mastery in that tongue.

Erasmus was the first writer who, disregarding national frontiers, addressed himself to all peoples, looking upon them as citizens of a single community — *mankind*. Masterpieces of the human mind are ultimately acclaimed by humanity and become an integral part of the heritage of civilized peoples; but as a rule, this process takes time, sometimes centuries. Erasmus was the first author to have as an audience *during his own lifetime,* and from the start, readers of the entire civilized world. His authority was as great in England as in Germany, in France as in Italy, in Switzerland as in Poland, in Spain as in Portugal, in Bohemia as in Hungary. His universality was accepted so naturally by his readers that they did not look upon him as a foreigner. Henry VIII in England, Francis I in France, Charles V in Spain, all the popes who succeeded to the Holy See during his life, offered Erasmus high positions. In this his case is unique. True, a nation had occasionally entrusted a high post to a foreigner. But Erasmus, a poor, rather ugly, frail little monk, was showered by offers not from one country but from *all* civilized countries and from the most powerful sovereigns.

In temperament and in taste this scholar Erasmus was a born artist. From childhood his avocation was painting. (See *Erasmus, Humanist and Painter* by M. Brockwell, 1918.) He had a keen awareness of form and color. In a convent at Delft, Holland, a religious painting — "Christ on the Cross" — executed by Erasmus in his youth was proudly pointed out for centuries. Not to speak of the manuscripts that he illuminated with flowers. But it was primarily as a writer that he was a painter. When, in his letters, he described an interior, a family, an inn, a city, he painted them with his pen, neglecting not the slightest picturesque or characteristic detail, in so impressive a fashion and in such vivid colors that the interiors and the many people live as though in a painting by Breughel, his compatriot, whose talent so resembled his own. Or he would devote several pages of a letter to tracing the psychological and physical portrait of a single man. These portraits are real masterpieces. One could rightly compare those of Henry VIII or Sir Thomas More, which he occasionally drew with his pen, in writing as fine and regular as though engraved by drypoint — that of an artist rather than a writer — with the portraits of Hans Holbein the younger. Read, for example, the long letter to Ulrich von Hutten who had asked Erasmus to describe Thomas More; then examine the remarkable portrait of this same friend by Holbein — and you will be struck by the resemblance between the two portraits, except that the one by Erasmus is enriched by intellectual, moral, biographical, and environmental characteristics which the brush of the great artist naturally could not communicate.

In his private life, the slightest lack of harmony, the slightest discord in proportion, color, or form, upset his stomach, just as the fish and eggs, which he execrated to the point of hysteria, made him suffer psychically. When he was old and suffering from stomach ulcers and kidney stones, or from articular and other pains, he would make a wide detour just to avoid a street that was not to his taste. In spite of the financial penury against which he had to fight for three-quarters of his life, he indulged in real extravagance to satisfy his tastes. He disliked stoves because of the smoke, the very thought of which nauseated him. Consequently, for warmth he drank the choicest burgundy, to which he attributed the virtue of keeping him alive; and he wrapped himself in fine and marvelously matched furs.

These, like the texture and lining of his robes, or the silken and embroidered tapestries on his room's walls, were the delight of the artists who repeatedly portrayed him. None of his contemporaries was painted more often by the most famous artists of the time — Holbein, Dürer,

Matsys. And of none do we preserve an iconography as rich as that of Erasmus.

In his esthetic revelings, he admitted no compromise. He even ordered his candles sent from Italy because of their color and shape. At a time when regular postal transportation did not exist, to order things from a foreign country made them so costly that one virtually had to be rich to satisfy such tastes. And Erasmus was for most of his life a beggar.

This man, a poised and methodical worker, with one of the best-balanced brains in history, was innately restless. A vagabond by nature, Erasmus was incapable of staying in one place for long. Fever for travel was characteristic of the cultivated men of his time; but Erasmus carried it further than most of his contemporary humanists. In spite of his continued poverty; in spite of the inconveniences, fatigues, and difficulties of the shortest journey, which we can scarcely imagine today — not to speak of the dangers incurred at a time when the roads seemed to be infested by brigands and robbers, who once nearly assassinated him — Erasmus continually changed residence, moving on with his manuscripts and his books, from city to city, from country to country, under all sorts of pretexts. The pretext of the money he hoped to acquire elsewhere more easily than where he was; the pretext of visiting libraries where, it is true, he made sensational discoveries, some of which put an indelible seal on his work and his time; the pretext of contagion, of which he had a real fear and which forced him to flee as far as his health and his means would permit, whenever an epidemic or the specter of one appeared, or whenever the number of funeral cars seemed to increase in the place where he was staying.

This fear of contagion and of death was an essential characteristic of Erasmus — one of which his reader should never lose sight. If it is not taken into account, not only his conduct in certain cases but the exact meaning of some of his most inspired pages may escape us. One of the most courageous men of all time, intellectually and morally, Erasmus was, physically, an avowed coward. He did not hide this nor did he attempt to defend himself. When a friend, writing from Paris which Erasmus had fled to avoid an epidemic, joked about his cowardice, Erasmus replied sharply: "If I were a Swiss mercenary soldier I ought to challenge you to a duel. But as I am only a poet, I hope you will permit me to laugh at your reproach."

Indeed, his profession as writer and critic of his time required an entirely different kind of courage, and the latter he had in abundance. He explained himself with such moving dignity that even the description of his physical cowardice has given us some fine pages on true heroism. Only the mind, he said, acting in spite of fear, is truly capable of courage. "If I am inclined to a thoughtful prudence," we read in his *Little Night Studies* (*Lucubratiunculae*), "if my nature is more delicate, am I a coward for that? It is not in my power to prevent my face from turning pale when a terrifying thing appears before my eyes. On the other hand, I could master my anguish so that not even the danger of certain death could turn me from what I considered to be right. . . . Is a man courageous only when he is foolhardy, scaling walls, rushing blindly into danger? Only he who knows how to be master of himself, who desires good for him who wishes him evil, who blesses him who curses him — only he deserves to be called courageous and magnanimous." Obsessed by the fear of his own death, which he constantly anticipated and frequently predicted, he was also inspired by it in his deeply moving interpretation of the agony of Jesus in the Garden of Gethsemane. So he longed for sudden death, of which he would have no foreknowledge. This scandalized orthodox Catholics. And yet Erasmus, the avowed coward, would doubtless have joined his friends on the scaffold rather than renounce his convictions — just as he accepted poverty rather than alienate his physical and moral independence.

Luther, out of gratitude to the German princes who had protected him against Rome, smothered in blood the only revolution that the German people in the course of history had dared to wage against their oppressors; but Erasmus, who was a court favorite and an unbridled flatterer, never lost his critical sense and never made the slightest moral concession to rulers. It was not only in his works that he unceasingly condemned their ways, their tyrannical methods of governing, exploiting the people for their own profit, and provoking wars, but every time he spoke of people of this caste, he revealed the infinite scorn which he felt for them. The kindness toward himself of kings, princes, and their entourage never turned his head; he always kept his balance. He answered politeness by politeness, he conformed to the etiquette of courts when he was present; but he avoided them like the plague as far as possible, always with the most perfect civility. Nothing is more characteristic of this attitude than a letter addressed to a friend who, called to the court of Charles V, sought advice on how to behave when he got there. This is how Erasmus summed up the so-called philosophy of life at royal courts: "Up to the age of fifty, I observed not a few things at princely courts, so that you can profit by my experience. Do not trust anyone who claims to be your friend. Let him smile, promise, embrace you and make as many promises as he likes. Do not believe in the sincere attachment of any of these people, and do not be in haste to trust anyone. Be polite to everyone. Politeness costs nothing. Bow, step back so that they can pass, and do not forget to call these gentlemen by their titles. Praise them effusively, promise generously. Select the role that you would like to play and never betray your real feelings. Adapt your grimaces to your words and your words to your grimaces. That is the philosophy of life at court. No one is qualified for it until he is totally freed of his capacity for shame and while he is not sufficiently trained to lie without wincing. . . . When I see how far you profit by my advice, I will initiate you into the deeper mysteries!"

Was Erasmus ungrateful — as some interested critics have claimed — when he accepted favors without renouncing an iota of his independence and of his freedom to criticize? Nonsense! Even at the peak of his fame, when he was no longer dependent on favors, he continued to speak of his former benefactors, crediting them with his triumphs and the best of his work. He had to a supreme degree what the French call *la reconnaissance du ventre,* and, aside from his natural goodness, he was inspired by the memory of these kindnesses when his turn came to help young scholars and writers. But when he was poverty-stricken, he had the courage and the pride to refuse certain offers at a time when his whole future was at stake. For he knew as well how to accept gifts — and even charity — with dignity as to refuse them with tact and humility. When, as an old man, he provided a young protégé who was going to England with letters of recommendation to his friends, he gave him some advice which reflected the wide experience of his youth in the art of begging and refusing: "They (the English) are generous and they will offer you presents, but remember the saying: Not everything, everywhere, and from everyone."

"I am as poor as a rat," he wrote at the age of thirty-four to a friend who urged him to accept a job; "but as you know, I must be free and I will be." And a little later he wrote again, "No rock could be as bare as I am now" — but he preferred his bareness to the sacrifice of a scrap of his time and freedom.

What his prejudiced critics called ingratitude was rather a form of heroism. As one of his English biographers said, Erasmus was a wild bird, willing to be caressed but refusing to sing in a cage. Liberty was essential to him, and he admired his benefactors at a distance. Their encouragement at close hand often killed his energy instead of giving it wings; although he could not get along without patrons, he preferred the freedom of a beggar to accepting a job or any offer which would put him under obligation.

5.

The Writer

ERASMUS WAS OFTEN ACCUSED of flattery and hypocrisy because, it was said, he did not have the courage to speak his own mind openly and under all circumstances. His adversaries claimed that he demolished the fortified position of others without even making clear his own. When Luther saw that Erasmus disliked him and his new creed and that no more help could be expected from him, he called him vindictively "The king of ambiguity." How sound are these grave charges?

Let us examine first the charge of ambiguity. We must bear in mind that Erasmus lived in an age when the stake and the gallows were the common lot of those who dared to speak the full truth. And Erasmus wanted not only to speak it but to make it widely known. For that reason he often used allusion and innuendo, of which he was a master and which, together with his wit, in certain phases of his struggle, formed a part of his strategical maneuverings. Compared, however, with other great writers of the sixteenth century — Sir Thomas More in his *Utopia,* Rabelais, Montaigne, and so forth — Erasmus was a virtuoso of precision; otherwise his lifework would have been valueless. It is true that we must often catch his real thought by reading between the lines, but no plain writing could be clearer than what he left to the imagination of the average reader. In the final analysis, nothing that was important to him remained obscure. And this applies even to problems the outlines of which might well have been blurred in clouds of metaphysics. There is broad daylight in his work. Even in his theological writings he never reasons in abstractions; the concreteness of his ideas, arguments, and criticisms is remarkably sculptural, both in his letters and in the bulk of his work.

And what a work! That immense body consists of 226 titles! If one were to include the successive editions which he constantly enriched and enlarged; his translations from the Greek authors, sacred and profane; the works of the Latin authors and Fathers of the Church which he edited and for which he wrote extensive commentaries and prefaces; and his revolutionary and daring translation of the New Testament, which was particularly dear to him and marked the peak of his fame — then one would obtain the number of five thousand!

Indeed, he was proficient in nearly all the fields of literature, and it is a pity that he never tried his hand in the domain of the theater. His sketchy *Julius Exclusus* is an excellent pattern of what he might have done. For in dialogue his style is that of the natural human voice. He liked dialogue and often used it even in his letters. In telling his correspondents of his meetings and his adventures with people of all kinds — even with servants — he switches suddenly from description to dialogue and paints his characters through their own words, through the exchange of a few typical phrases. Indeed, his letters as a whole are a rich gallery of contemporary portraits, and the most striking are those in which portraiture is achieved through dialogue. While reading such letters, one feels that Erasmus has captured not only the physical and moral features of the most diversified people of his time but their living voices, and his own as well.

(Erasmus' great gift for these dialogues as well as their extraordinary lively form — throughout his whole work — deserve a special study. As far as I can ascertain, no author has yet attempted to analyze the art of Erasmus from a purely theatrical point of view, in spite of the great indebtedness of the stage to him. Preserved Smith, author of the best American biography of Erasmus, in his *A Key to the "Colloquies" of Erasmus*, points rightly at the nearly unique influence, in the history of world literature, of the dialogues of Erasmus on the greatest authors and playwrights of the last four centuries. Some of them — for instance, Rabelais, Fontenelle, Voltaire, and Walter Scott — frankly admitted it. Others, although borrowing generously from Erasmus, failed to acknowledge it; the most illustrious names in this category are Montaigne, Cervantes, Shakespeare, Ben Jonson, Molière. Says Preserved Smith: "All these heirs and imitators of Erasmus bear witness to the *incomparable* vitality of his art." Indeed, as in many other fields, Erasmus remains still the master of the modern dialogue form.)

By instinct a judge of men, he not only understood others but he understood himself — a rare quality in a man so generally admired. He even knew his own limitations, which is even rarer in a writer, particularly one whose works were everywhere in demand, whatever the subject, and whose advice was sought by the most powerful men on earth. Even the adversaries who so severely criticized his works could not deny his extraordinary flair. Instead they declared — as one of his present-day partisan critics has also done — that he owed his enormous influence less to the quality of his ideas than to his unusual psychological gifts, which enabled him to impose his opinions on his century. "His wit and his knowledge of human nature made him the dictator of intellectual Europe." (Cf. *The Youth of Erasmus* by Albert Hyma.)

If, in the final analysis, when we know the real facts of his life and work, the reproach of ambiguity vanishes, it still remains true that he liked to flatter and that, with his enticing, natural friendliness, he knew how to flatter. In doing so, he conformed to the rules of his century, which was one of the most polite in history. But even in the most unbridled flattery, he never sacrificed the higher truth. It might be said that his excessive praise of kings actually increased his independence, enabling him to criticize and to condemn them as a class, and to express his thoughts with the greatest possible freedom. He even said as much himself. In the preface and conclusion to his *Panegyric on Philip the Fair,* he declares openly that by flattery he sought a definite goal. In order to appreciate the courage of such an avowal, one must recall that at the time of the publication of the *Panegyric,* his career as a writer was just beginning, and he did not yet enjoy that immunity which his fame was later to procure for him. Yet in his conclusion, he explains once and for all what value must be attached to his flatteries. Those who accused him of it later on, when he was waging his heroic battle openly, ought to have remembered this — unless they were resolved to discredit him at any price because they were incapable of parrying his blows.

Here are a few characteristic passages from this significant conclusion, which was published in the form of a letter to Johannes Paludanus of the University of Louvain. Paludanus was a distinguished scholar and an influential person in public life. It was at his suggestion that the government ordered Erasmus to compose and deliver the official *Panegyric* in the name of the country, and it was he who urged him to publish this fine piece of rhetoric.

Those who think that panegyrics are nothing but flattery [the author declared] seem unaware of the purpose for which this type of literature was invented by men of great wisdom. By placing before their eyes the picture of virtue, these authors were trying to make bad princes better, to encourage the good, to instruct the ignorant, to set on the right path those who were in error, to stimulate the hesitating, to recall even the lost to some feeling of shame.

Is it indeed to be supposed that a philosopher of the quality of Calisthenes in praising Alexander, or of Lysias, or Isocrates, or Pliny, or a host of other moralists, devoted themselves to this type of composition with any other purpose than an exhortation to virtue under the pretext of praise? . . . Did not the Apostle Paul sometimes have recourse to this pious adulation, praising people in order to make them better? Tell me by what means you could reprove the cruelty of a wicked sovereign with less risk and more severity than by praising his so-called clemency? How could you hold up his rapacity, his violence, his lust to public scorn better than by praising his benevolence, his moderation, his chastity? . . . Plato and the Stoics permitted a wise man to have recourse to a salutary lie. Do we not at times rightly encourage children to love virtue by being prodigal with unmerited praise? Is not the best doctor he who tells his patients that their symptoms and their appearance are just what he could wish, not because it is the truth but in the hope of making it so? . . .

Certainly I have attempted to draw up the plan and composition of the whole speech in such a way as to make clear to the cultivated and attentive listener that flattery was the last thing I had in view. No one could vouch better than you for the fact that this vice has always revolted me, that I would scarcely be capable of adulating anyone even if I wanted to, nor desirous of doing so if I were capable of it. That is why I do not fear that such an imputation can be attached to my character in the mind of those who, like you, know Erasmus inside and out . . .

"Cultivated and attentive" readers of Erasmus could not, in all honesty, be mistaken as to the meaning of his flatteries. That Europe understood him perfectly is shown by the fact that he was venerated as the "Prince of the Humanists" by the most advanced minds in every country. That the Holy See and its inquisitorial agencies abroad understood him equally well appears in the fact that when Erasmus was dead and they no longer feared his pen or hoped that he could be useful to them in their struggle against Luther, they put many of his works on the Index and forbade Catholics to read them — a ruling which, in spite of the strictures of the Church, has been, as the French say, no more than a sword-thrust in

water. It is true that the most feared inquisitorial court of
Spain — the famous Holy Office of the Inquisition, assembled
in Valladolid — and that of Louvain in the Low Countries
and elsewhere, as well as the mighty theological faculty of
the Paris University, did not wait so long to inquire into
his heresies and to condemn solemnly his books to be burnt,
particularly *Peace Protests!, Colloquies,* and *Praise of Folly*
which disturbed them most. However, none of the popes
or the kings of those countries, as long as Erasmus lived,
ever allowed those condemnations to be put into effect. All
this changed as soon as their author was dead. Erasmus'
works were tried again. This time an even greater number
of them were condemned and their author cursed more
vigorously than ever before.

It is interesting to recall the text in which, six years after
the death of Erasmus, the Sorbonne, for centuries the most
authoritative mouthpiece of Catholic theology, expressed
triumphantly its definite condemnation of *Praise of Folly:*
"In composing *Praise of Folly,* Erasmus revealed himself to
be mad and insane, even impious, injurious to God, to Jesus
Christ, to the Virgin, to the Saints, to ceremonies, to theologians, to beggar monks whom he insulted with a corrupt
and blasphemous mouth," and consequently this work must
be suppressed forever, "lest those who read it become mad
and insane and finally heretics."

In spite of the terrible weapons of the Inquisition and the
threat of excommunication, this did not halt the brilliant and
perhaps unique career of the immortal satire on the folly
of men. After the death of Erasmus, and in Latin alone, fifty-
eight editions appeared in the sixteenth century; thirty-eight
in the seventeenth, sixty-two in the eighteenth, and some fifty
during the nineteenth century, not to mention the innumerable editions of translations which are constantly reprinted
in all civilized languages.

There is an amusing sidelight on *Praise of Folly* having

been put upon the Index. Some years after the First World War, one of the great Parisian newspapers took a poll of its readers on the origins of journalism; the purpose was to find a saint for journalists, since all the other professions in Catholic countries had one. The overwhelming majority of votes were cast for Erasmus. The French were quite right: among so many other titles to fame, he can indeed claim that of father of modern journalism. When this choice had been made, the journalists proclaimed him their patron: "Saint Erasmus, pray for us!" Of course, this lay canonization was only a joke, and history, frequently so lugubrious, was smiling ironically through the French spiritual descendants of the author of the *Folly*. But this irony would have pleased Erasmus who delighted in laughing and in arousing laughter.

Soon after, in 1935, Sir Thomas More was canonized by the Church of Rome on the occasion of the four hundredth anniversary of his execution by Henry VIII. In a way, that was also the canonization of Erasmus. More was his closest and dearest friend; they regarded themselves as having a single soul. On learning of More's martyrdom, Erasmus said that he no longer feared death and had only one desire: to rejoin his friend. This wish was granted and he died scarcely a year after the martyrdom of More.

It was in More's house that Erasmus composed *Praise of Folly*, it was to More that he dedicated it, and — in his immortal preface — it was to More that he confided its defense. No one else defended the author and his *Folly* with the passion and devotion of More, who five years later published his own *Utopia*. For decades he was Erasmus' most enthusiastic ally and disciple in his fight for peace, for democracy, for the internal reform of the Church of Rome, as well as in his crusade against the customs of the times in the monastic orders, in the clergy, and in the highest ranks of those who held the power and privilege of canonizing saints. Now he is Saint Thomas More! And through him, this sanctity sheds its soft light on the condemned author of *Folly*. And that is only just. As P. S. Allen said in *The Age of Erasmus:* "In his dreams of what he would do with his life, he had ever seen himself advancing not the name of Erasmus but the glory of God."

Erasmus is indeed the father of modern journalism. No one could reasonably contest this title, which he owes principally to his letters. At an age when newspapers did not exist and few nations sent diplomatic representatives abroad, Erasmus' letters, printed and made public in all countries, with or without his consent, played an essential role in international, political, and religious life. Their extraordinary success is explained not only by his genius as a writer or even by the value that was attached to his opinions, but by the fact that no one in Europe was better informed on current events and on the intrigues and the crimes that were plotted behind the scenes of the day. In constant touch by letter with every country and with people of all classes from kings and popes to the humblest priest and scholar, he heard at his writing desk the echo of actions or plans for action. Shut up at home, he heard so distinctly the cacophony of the world that he need not have envied our modern radio. No statesman, no high dignitary of the Roman Church could have had as complete a picture of international daily life as Erasmus, and it was through his letters that people in various countries learned of it. Along with the facts, there were perspicacious commentaries, so full of wisdom that political professionals could gather invaluable suggestions.

We will never know whether the publication of certain letters *without his knowledge* — as he vehemently complained — was in every case *against his wishes*. We do know that his continued ill health — real as it was — often served as an excuse when he wanted to get rid of undesirable visitors;

or when he did not choose to visit important people, or serve as arbitrator on the Councils of Augsburg or at Worms to make historical decisions in the Lutheran affair. In the same way, it seems to me, by posing as the victim of an abuse of confidence or of theft, he was able to use his letters as potent weapons.

He lived in a violent and perfidious time when extravagant means were necessary if one were to make the truth heard without running too great risk. We cannot judge the proceedings of an inquisitorial age by the standards of our own epoch. The best men of that time constantly employed such methods. Sir Thomas More, not daring to publish his *Utopia* in England although he occupied a high government post, confided the manuscript to Erasmus, who took it to Antwerp and had it printed by his friend Peter Gilles — to whom the author dedicated the first edition. When this work appeared in 1516, Thomas More protested indignantly — as, for example, in his letter to Warham, Primate of England and Archbishop of Canterbury — that he had never intended to make public these lucubrations, written for his own amusement, and that he was the victim of a revolting betrayal of confidence. But at the same time he showered Erasmus and Gilles with proofs of his gratitude. The important thing in this maneuver was to strike the blow, and that he did in good time. Why should Erasmus, a better strategist and perhaps even more intelligent than More, have scrupled to resort to the same practice? It may even have been he who suggested this plan to the author of *Utopia*.

It is thus more or less certain that these so-called "indiscretions" were for the most part desired and managed by Erasmus himself. The goal was worth the effort. If he attacked a man of high position or flattered him, to make him malleable and more accessible to an idea that he was suggesting for the public good, but doubted the efficacy of his confidential exhortation, he did not scruple to make his letter public through the help of someone to whom he simultaneously communicated a copy. He was ready to excuse himself to the recipient, claiming either the scandalous indiscretion of a messenger or the work of a thief who had taken the copy kept for his secret files. Thousands of copies of these letters were distributed throughout Europe, crystallizing large bodies of opinion and ideas. One can imagine that often the recipient of the letter had no choice but to renounce the sinister projects revealed by Erasmus or to yield to the pressure of international opinion and do what his correspondent demanded. In other words, Erasmus' letters became the most enlightened expressions of public opinion at a time when there was no press to form or to echo it.

Nonetheless, it would be a mistake to consider the letters of Erasmus only from the purely opportunist, political, or journalistic angle. He wrote many of a totally different character, probably hundreds of thousands, of which the greater part have unhappily been lost. He wrote with affection to friends, scattered in many countries, with whom he maintained close relations. He wrote to defend himself against attack, or to attack on a more restrained scale than he did in his books. But for the most part he wrote, one might say, by *vocation*. In a remarkable analysis that he made in his old age of his own literary talent, he complained that he had spent most of his life composing works under the pressure of events; he concluded that it was not in these that his personality had found the most adequate means of expression and that if he had had freedom to choose the one most appropriate to his gifts, he would have expressed himself in some other form. *His real gift,* he declared, *consisted in writing letters.*

The truth is that he wrote them with delight, sometimes as many as thirty in a day, often containing several thousand words. It is not rare to find among them specimens of ten or even fifteen thousand words, like that to "Grunnius" quoted above. With those of Cicero and of Voltaire, these letters are doubtless the most remarkable of their kind, and their authors will be known by them long after their other works have been forgotten. Those of Erasmus are real masterpieces, which, aside from their intrinsic — historical, biographical, literary — value, cast a fascinating light over all his other works. This enormous quantity of work produced by a single man staggers us, particularly when we recall that this puny little monk, barely five feet tall, worked, in spite of his aches and pains, eighteen hours a day, standing before his desk. Most of this time was consecrated to his letters, at a time when a regular postal service did not exist and each letter had to be sent by a messenger whose long journey must be paid for. They were the delight of his friends and his contemporaries, even when they did not deal with immediate questions. They were copied simply for their beauty, they were passed from hand to hand, manuscript collections were made of them, and, as there was no copyright even within the countries where the author lived, they were finally printed. Erasmus in the end decided to make his own collections and to publish them with a preface. These collections were snatched up and reprinted each time with new additions and often with new prefaces.

P. S. Allen, the English scholar who devoted fifty years to collecting these letters — discovering unknown ones, correcting the text of those already published, and providing them with a host of valuable commentary — has brought out the most complete and accurate collection up to this time. He died before the appearance of the eighth volume, but after having carried his gigantic work to its end. His wife, Mrs. H. M. Allen, herself a remarkable Latinist — whose name, beginning with the third volume, appeared on the title page with that of her husband — concluded the publication (*Opus Epistolarum Des. Erasmi Roterodami*, edited by P. S. Allen and H. M. Allen, 11 vols., Oxford, 1906 to 1947). Thanks to the Allens, we now have all the known letters from Erasmus as well as the ones that he received and that throw light on his own. This monumental work is the most remarkable of all the enormous literature concerning Erasmus, containing all the discoveries made about him in four centuries by hundreds of authors. Henceforth, the name of Allen is so linked with that of Erasmus that it will be impossible to advance in any study of his works, life, character, or even his times and his contemporaries, without having first delved into this infinitely rich mine.

6.

His Struggle for Peace

ONE CAN DISTINGUISH two definite periods in Erasmus' struggle for peace. In the first, he denounced war and those who waged it. In the second, no longer satisfied with denunciations and curses, he passed on to constructive criticism, indicating methods that would assure permanent peace. This project — for it amounted to one — was not developed all at once. He advanced step by step, elaborating the details, until the day came when he condensed them in impressive and lapidary form in his little work *Peace Protests!*

To declare that aggressive war was a crime and that aggressors were criminals, he did not wait until he was famous to express himself fearlessly. As early as 1504, in his *Panegyric on Philip the Fair,* he dared to tell the man who was his sovereign, and — through the marriage with the daughter of the Catholic Kings — heir to the crown of Spain, that nothing could so dishonor a prince as war, just as nothing could make him so beloved by his people and by God as to preserve peace by every conciliatory and unselfish method. (So far as I could ascertain, this work has never been translated.)

Erasmus returned to this subject three years later in his *Declamation Against War (Antipolemus),* which, written in 1507, was lost and never published. He wrote it shortly after his arrival in Bologna. There, involuntarily, he had ocular evidence of what was, to his eyes, a shocking scandal — the triumphant entry of Pope Julius II at the head of his victorious armies. As Erasmus was already a person of considerable importance in Europe — although only seven years had passed since he published his first major work, the *Adages* — Julius II asked him through the Cardinal of Saint-Georges to become his official trumpeter and to compose a *Declamation* to his military glory, justifying in advance the war which this successor of Saint Peter was planning to start against the Republic of Venice. The monk Erasmus obeyed and wrote not one but two *Declamations*. They were not, however, panegyrics on war but violent diatribes against it. He even went so far as to formulate the only conditions that could excuse war — an act as criminal as it was unchristian. Unhappily, these two works were lost. What little we know of them from the letters of Erasmus and from Melanchthon suffices to illustrate his courage in confronting the formidable Pope intoxicated by military victories.

From the moment when he saw Julius II carried under the canopy of a triumphant warrior, to the acclamations of his army and the clergy, and behaving like a true "Julius" — or, using a play on words, as a "Second Julius" (alluding to Julius Caesar), as Erasmus remarked ironically in one of his letters — he felt such disgust that he never recovered from it. And as Julius II, not satisfied by the victories he had already won and in spite of the warnings of our author, began his ruthless war against the Venetians, Erasmus henceforth never missed an opportunity to pillory that Pope. His first attack dates from 1509, two years after the scandalous incident at Bologna.

That year, returning from a long visit to Italy, he hurried to London where he had been called by the new king, Henry VIII. After crossing the Alps and a great part of Europe on horseback, he descended the Rhine by boat from Strassburg, crossed the Channel, and arrived in London in record time. He was at once exhausted and happy to stay with his good friend Thomas More. Scarcely settled down, he had an acute attack of kidney stones, from which he had been suffering for a year. In the state of medicine at that time there was no relief from his pain, but Erasmus had his own remedy. When he had these attacks, he concentrated so completely on another subject that everything else, including his own body, became unreal. So he shut himself up in More's library with some good burgundy wine and set to work writing *Praise of Folly*. At the end of seven days — probably the duration of his attack — the book was ready. It is the gayest of all his works. And the naughtiest too. Perhaps we owe the violence of his sarcasm to the degree of violence of his pain. The more he suffered the more he must have attempted to smother the attack on his own poor body in a laugh which would soon shake all Europe.

Praise of Folly was a settlement of his accounts with all those who dishonored the Church, science, humanity — the unworthy monks, theologians, priests, bishops, cardinals, popes, kings. Many pages are devoted to the scourge of war and those who foment and wage it. The place of honor among the latter was reserved for the popes.

Reading this work, one becomes aware of the moral evolution of the Church of Rome since that time. The popes of today are no longer warriors but pastors who abhor war and preach peace, and their words would be among the finest with which any pacifist anthology could be adorned. But at the time of Erasmus, and for many years before and after his day, many of them were warriors and persecutors whose scandalous behavior hurt the conscience of those whose only desire was for the purity of the faith, founded on peace and love among men. Thus Erasmus, in his satire, slapped them publicly as no one before him had ever dared to do. The Church of Rome owes Erasmus a bright candle, for these great changes are due in part to his public denunciations of scandalous ecclesiastical behavior, although it is also true that the denunciation of these same grievances originated the reform movements of that period.

What a pity that publishers, who continually reprint *Praise of Folly,* are satisfied with translations that are several centuries old and no longer reflect the power of its pages, which are so astonishingly modern. I am aware that in 1941 and 1946 American scholars brought out exact translations. But, as Erasmus himself pointed out, an exact translation is not necessarily a faithful one; the latter requires the hand of a writer who, by substituting contemporary terminology for obsolete phrases, might rejuvenate the laughter of Erasmus and delight our epoch, which is so rich in subjects for satire and so poor in satirical authors.

How the indignation of our little monk rang out, clearly audible over his roars of laughter! In the following passage he lashes out at the warlike Pope, Julius II, speaking cautiously of "popes" but in such a way that everyone recognized his real target:

Although Saint Peter says in the Gospels to his divine master, "We have left everything to follow you," the popes claim a patrimony of lands, cities, taxes, principalities; and when, animated by truly Christian zeal, they use iron and fire to protect this dear patrimony, when their paternal and holy arms shed the blood of Christians, it is then, proud of having felled these unfortunates whom they call the enemies of the Church, that they boast of fighting for it and defending this bride of Jesus Christ with an altogether apostolic courage. But they do not dream that the most baneful enemies of the Church are the bad popes, who by their silence let Jesus Christ be forgotten, who traffic shamelessly in indulgences, corrupt his doctrine by far-fetched interpretations, and destroy it entirely by the contagious example of their abominable profligacy.

Because the Church of Jesus Christ was built by blood, ratified by blood and augmented by blood, they believe that it is necessary to shed blood to govern and defend it — as though Jesus Christ no longer existed, or were no longer able to protect his own as he has always done! They know that war is so cruel a thing that it is more fitting for wild beasts than for men; so furious that the Furies themselves, according to the poets, spewed it upon the earth; so baneful that it drags in its wake the most frightful disorders; so unjust that it is ordinarily provoked only by the most infamous brigands; so impious that it is entirely contrary to Jesus Christ; and yet these vicars of a God of peace neglect all other occupations to devote themselves entirely to this abominable art.

Sometimes one sees decrepit old men affect the vigor of young men in these wars, pouring out huge sums to support them, exposing themselves with tireless ardor to all the labor they require, unscrupulously overturning laws, religion, peace, until at length they become the scourges of the human race. Is it believable that there are adroit flatterers who dare give this obvious madness the fine name of zeal, piety and courage, and who employ all the subtlety of their minds to prove that he who draws his sword and plunges it into the breast of his brother may nonetheless retain in his heart that perfect charity for his neighbor that Jesus Christ so recommended to his disciples!

I am still uncertain whether the popes set the example for certain German bishops or whether they took it from them. However it may be, the latter are not so particular; they do not wear all these episcopal decorations, they do not entertain themselves by benedictions and other ceremonies of that kind; but they dress and behave like real satraps, believing that it is shameful and unworthy for a bishop to return his strong and courageous soul to God elsewhere than on the battlefield.

With the publication of *Praise of Folly* in 1511 practically ends the period in which Erasmus confined himself, in his fight for peace, to a criticism of war and those who wage it. When he returned to the charge, in 1514, he reappeared with a new strategy and new weapons. Henceforth his criticism included, along with his vehement condemnations of this crime against humanity, a constructive program of peace which he continued to expand in the series of works which followed in rapid succession. At the same time he sought allies and strengthened the ground on which to launch his battle with the greatest chance of success.

The hour which seemed most propitious for starting this crusade struck while he was at Cambridge, where for several years he had occupied a chair as professor. He was smothered there. The narrow, bigoted university atmosphere weighed heavily on this genial vagabond accustomed to breathing the air of the artistic and intellectual centers of Europe. This residence at Cambridge became the more insupportable when he realized that his project was well advanced but that he could not carry it out unless he was on the Continent. There only, in the immediate neighborhood of the key men on whom the fate of the peoples depended, would he be able to deploy his activity effectively. Besides, in spite of the war which was raging in England between Henry VIII and James of Scotland, and the one which had set at odds the king of England and Louis XII of France, the time must have seemed ideal for opening his campaign for peace — a conviction which was strengthened during the two following years.

In 1515, Francis I mounted the throne of France at the age of twenty-one. In 1516, Charles of Austria, only sixteen years old, became the ruler of Spain, the Dukedom of Burgundy and thus of the Netherlands, the recently discovered America, and, three years later, of the immense Holy Roman or German Empire. These kings were young, they were free, they had not yet had time to bind themselves by treaties that they would be forced to keep in case of war. Nor had they yet had time to adopt a definite foreign policy to which their names were attached. Power had not yet corrupted them and their consciences were clear.

It is true that Henry VIII, though also very young, had already dipped his hands in blood. But as his adversary, Louis XII, was dead, his reconciliation with the young king of France would be easy; for the moment, no personal animosity as yet divided them. Moreover, not only was Erasmus friendly with Henry VIII, sought after by Francis I, admired by Leo X, who had succeeded the hated Julius II on the throne of Saint Peter; but also he had just been appointed by Charles V, as soon as the latter mounted the throne, to the post of state councillor. This was an honorary post, simply an excuse for giving Erasmus a pension that would free him from his eternal worries about money. But at the same time the new dignity placed him in the young monarch's intimacy. Jealous of his liberty, Erasmus hesitated before accepting, and agreed only when he was assured that he could keep his complete independence with respect to the king and government.

He was, then, entitled to be hopeful. With his prestige and his eloquence he might lead these young crowned heads along the irresistible current of his dreams, proceed with them to the realization of his ideas of peace — working together for the happy future of humanity. Erasmus' optimism was entirely justified. He was not one of those dreamers who engage in a crusade without having first weighed all the chances of success. An idealist in his ideas and in his dreams, Erasmus was realistic when it came to carrying them out.

Erasmus left Cambridge in 1514. War was raging between England and Scotland and it was important to act without losing another moment. He conceived the idea of writing a work on peace. But time was short, and he decided to inaugurate his crusade by a letter to Antony Bergen, the abbot of Saint-Bertin. Before crossing the channel and immediately after his arrival in London, he wrote to this man, whom he chose after long reflection. He could not have done better. Indeed, Antony Bergen had more influence than any other churchman at the various courts of Europe, particularly that of Emperor Maximilian and his grandson Charles, who was soon to become the most powerful monarch of Christendom.

Erasmus had long known Antony Bergen, having accepted some help from him in his early days, and, as an eminent Latinist, assisted him in writing letters, particularly one to Cardinal Giovanni de Medici, now Pope Leo X. However, the man who wrote to Antony Bergen after so many years was no longer the little monk who had sought charity from the rich and powerful abbot, but the great Erasmus whose name rang through all Europe and who sought to enroll the abbot in the service of the cause to which he was going to devote himself. And, through Antony Bergen as intermediary, Erasmus was addressing himself to the Emperor Maximilian to whom, he knew, his letter would be shown. Anyhow, to be certain of this, he made the letter public as soon as he had sent it.

This letter, too long to be quoted here in its entirety, contains the seed of all the fundamental ideas on peace that Erasmus was later to develop in his political works. But from now on he was no longer satisfied merely to condemn war: he begins to suggest means of preventing it. For this reason, he violently attacks the kings and princes who so often forgot that the domains they governed were not their private property. He warns them bluntly that, contrary to their opinion, it is not military conquests which determine the stability of empires and thrones but the consent of the people governed — and the latter crave peace. So his letter was an unequivocal warning to Maximilian, who was building an empire by wars and by princely marriages. And it was also a defiance hurled at the pope and the higher clergy, reminding them that their role and their function were primarily to make peace and good will reign on earth, instead of being benevolent spectators of wars, encouraging them, or even waging wars themselves. If the authority of the popes must be manifested outside the domain of spiritual power, it should only be for the purpose of preventing bloodshed, only to impose peace on earth, as effectively as Julius

II, abusing his authority, had succeeded in imposing war. Here, for the first time, Erasmus suggests the principle of international arbitration to which he summons all nations:

I see great movements arising. . . . May the favor of God calm this tempest in Christendom. . . . I often wonder what drives — I will not say Christians — but *men* to exterminate one another like madmen at the price of such effort, such expense, and such risks. What do we do all our life long but wage war? Not even all animals fight, except some wild species. And even they fight not among themselves but with animals of a different species. Besides, they fight with their natural weapons and not with machines in the invention of which we employ an ingenuity worthy of the devils. . . .

Consider also how many crimes are committed under the pretext of war, when, as they say, arms speak and the laws are silent; how many thefts, how many sacrilegious acts, how many rapes, how many other abuses which one is ashamed to name! And this moral contagion lasts for many years after the war is over. If one calculates the expenses of a war, one will see how much more one loses than gains, even when he is the victor. What kingdom that is won can compensate for the life and the blood of so many thousand people? And yet it is those who have nothing to do with the fighting who are the most bitterly afflicted by the evils of war.

The advantages of peace benefit everyone, but war makes even the victor weep. And it is accompanied by such a host of calamities that it verifies the fiction of the poets who say that war comes to us from hell and that it is sent by the Furies. And I am not speaking of the popular uprisings within states, which are productive of the most disastrous results.

If it is a desire for fame which leads us into the temptation to wage war, such fame cannot be the true kind, because it is sought principally by acts of injustice. It is far more glorious to found states than to destroy them. If gain is our objective, no war was ever ended so satisfactorily that it did not cause more harm than good to those engaged in it, and no sovereign can injure his enemy in war without, first, injuring his own subjects. Finally, when we see human affairs, like the ebb and flow of Euripus, subject to perpetual change and always confused, what is the advantage of exerting such effort to build an empire which, some day, after a great overturn, will pass into other hands? With how much blood the Roman Empire was built and how soon it began to crumble!

You will tell me that the rights of sovereigns should be upheld. It is not for me to speak carelessly of the actions of princes. I know only that excessive right is excessive injustice (*summum jus summa injuria*). There are princes who decide first what they want and then seek for pretexts to cloak the real motives for their warlike actions. But who, I wonder, among the great changes to which human affairs are subject, will ever lack a pretext?

Let us admit that there are real grounds for dispute. . . . Is it necessary to shed blood? . . . There are popes, bishops, wise men of unshakeable integrity who can regulate these small disputes without starting wars — always followed by other wars — and without bringing chaos to both divine and human things. It is the very function of the Roman Pontiff, of the cardinals, the bishops and abbots, to settle the disputes between Christian princes. It is for that purpose that they should use their authority! . . .

But, you will say, suppose that the other side refuses to submit to the decision of these well-meaning people; in that case what do you expect me to do? To that I reply: First, if you are a real Christian, I suggest that you bear and forbear, submerging your rights, whatever they may be. Second, if you are a wise man, I would urge you to calculate what it would cost to defend your rights. If the price is excessive — and it surely will be if you take to arms — do not insist on your rights, which, after all, may be unfounded, at a cost of so many miseries inflicted upon humanity, so many dead, so many orphans, so many tears. . . .

If rights there are which must be defended by arms, they can only be of the grosser kind, having the savor of a Christianity that is already degenerating, and weighed down with the burden of worldly goods. In this case, and in spite of the fact that war is not always disapproved of by pious authors when, to uphold our faith, Christian peace is defended against the invasion of barbarians — in that case, I say, I do not know whether I should approve of such wars. Why should we rely upon these — after all — only *human* authorities rather than on the many maxims of Christ, the Apostles, and the most orthodox and approved

Fathers of the Church, on peace and on the forgiveness of evils? Besides, what policy cannot be justified in some way? Particularly the policy of those who, having in their hands the conduct of affairs of state, are the very men whose crimes are praised by the flattery of so many people without a single one daring to criticize their mistakes, in spite of the fact that everyone knows the sighs, the longings, and the prayers for peace of reasonable people. And if you look closer you will see that generally it is personal interests of princes alone which cause wars. But, I ask you, do you think it is compatible with humanity that the world should constantly be upset from top to bottom by war for no other motive than because such-and-such a sovereign has some reason to complain of another, or perhaps only pretends to have?

We may hope for the best outcome but it will only be a hope. For my part, whatever fortune I may have lies in England. I would renounce it gladly if Christian peace could be established among Christians. This project would be greatly advanced if you were to assert your authority whose influence is so great over Prince Charles and still greater over Maximilian, while the English nobility is in sympathy with it. I have no doubt that you have already observed the great evils caused by war, even the warlike actions of your friends. That is why, by endeavoring to put an end to war, you would be serving your own interests . .

Once having written this letter, Erasmus, while continuing his most important works of exegesis and his struggle for the purification of religion and the Church, never abandoned world politics. He became the watchdog of peace, and it was from the standpoint of peace that he henceforth judged events and the men who promoted them.

While working on several political pamphlets and books, but without awaiting their publication, he addressed himself directly to the new pope Leo X, a year after having written to the abbot of Saint-Bertin. This time he expressed his horror not only of wars between Christian countries, but of war in general, even when waged against sworn enemies of Christianity. In the opinion of Erasmus, the princes were using the Turks only as a pretext in order to assuage their warlike instincts and their appetite for conquest. As a matter of fact, he declared, devotion to Christ's teachings should forbid rather than incite Christians to crusades. The only war to which Jesus and Paul exhorted their followers was against their own vices. Any other war, even in the name of Christ, was therefore unchristian. Besides, such wars can never be waged as successfully as by moral means. Indeed, no weapon would be more powerful to convert the Turks to Christianity than the example "of our own lives." Thus, instead of using violence to make disciples of Christ of those who follow the teachings of other masters, the Christian princes should first endeavor to be Christians themselves and to practice goodness, tolerance, universal peace. "In the same way," Erasmus goes on, "in which Christ himself with his apostles and martyrs have conquered the world by their kindliness, patience, holy teachings, so may we succeed in subduing the Turks by the purity of our own lives rather than by the strength of our arms. Thus the realm of Chris-tianity will be vindicated by the same means by which it was originally implanted."

Coming from Erasmus and addressed to the pope, this statement is the more remarkable because the Turks were actually invading Europe.

Then, with extraordinary audacity, the monk Erasmus ad-vised the pope not to let himself be tempted by the laurels of war like his bellicose predecessor. Let Leo X, he ex-claimed, seek his fame elsewhere, let him gather his laurels by imposing on Christendom not war but peace: "Let others celebrate by their praises the wars fomented or led success-fully by the Second Julius [always alluding to Julius Caesar]! Let others review his victories obtained by arms, and celebrate his triumphs worthy of emperors! Whatever his glory may be, even these people would be forced to admit that it is linked to infinite sufferings of multitudes of men."

To forestall a reply in phrases that would commit the

Pope to nothing, to force him to take steps to stop the
carnage, Erasmus immediately made this letter public.
Shielding himself behind the unbridled flatteries with which
he showered Leo X — as though paying homage to him before
the world — Erasmus stood before his Holy Father as the most
obedient of his sons. But humanistic Europe clearly understood his feelings and his purpose, and Erasmus' cry of conscience stirred all hearts that abhorred war.

When this letter had been made public, Erasmus openly
began his long-planned peace offensive. At the same time
he was working, under pressure, on his revolutionary edition
of the first printed Greek version of the New Testament —
editio princeps — which he collated from the best manuscripts
he could find, as well as on his no less revolutionary Latin
translation of the same, both of which he dedicated to Leo
X with the latter's consent. In this way he hoped to forestall those who might accuse him of having produced an impious and heretical work, as any deviation from Jerome's
translation, the Vulgate, was considered.

Erasmus took advantage of that publication to show in his
Introductions to the Gospels how their teachings are uncom-
promisingly opposed to war, and to define his own ideal of
peace in the light of the Scriptures. But he was anxious, too,
to restore the exact meaning to certain words, symbols, and
sayings, a meaning to which he had already referred in *Enchiridion*, and which, in his version, became even in one
place of the New Testament — as well as in various passages
of his own *Annotations* to it — unitarian rather than trinitar-
ian. (I refer to the passage I John V:7, which is the main
source for the doctrine about the Trinity. Not finding it in
the Greek manuscripts, not even in that of the Vatican, Erasmus simply omitted that sentence. To him it was no more
than an unfounded interpolation in Jerome's Vulgate.

See also Erasmus' *Annotations* on this passage as well as on
John I:1 and Romans IX:5. There is, in various languages,
a rich literature dealing with Erasmus' anti-trinitarian tendencies, which, however, he never openly admitted. The
reader will find references to some of those studies in the
remarkable *A History of Unitarianism* by Earl Morse Wil-
bur, Harvard University Press, 1946, 2nd printing, pp.
14-15.)

At the same time Erasmus was working on his *Institutio
Principis Christiani,* or *School for the Christian Prince,* which
was primarily a pacifist work, intended for Prince Charles
of Austria. It was also a year exceptionally rich in remarkable letters, a number of which have come down to us. But
Erasmus still found time to compose some little works, two
of which in particular — elements in his peace offensive — are
among the most important: his commentaries on two Latin
sayings, about *The Beetle and the Eagle* and *"War is sweet
to those who aren't fighting" (Dulce Bellum Inexpertis)* , a
phrase taken from Vegetius' book *De Re Militari* (Chapter
XIV). Very soon it became one of the most famous adages
of Erasmus himself.

It must be remembered that the *Adages* was his first printed
book and that it appeared in 1500, as though to inaugurate
the century. This work was written under unusual circumstances. When Erasmus was returning from his first visit
to England on his way to France, the English customs officers,
because of a law forbidding the exportation of gold, con-
fiscated all the money with which his friends in London had
provided him. Furious and penniless, he began, as soon as
he set foot on the ship, to think of some way of making money
in a hurry. As the Renaissance had restored to fashion the
literature of ancient Greek and Roman authors (and with
it the art of quotation) , up-to-date people, while submitting
to the caprices of fashion, were unable to satisfy them as easily
as usual, i.e. to acquire rapidly the knowledge they lacked.

Consequently, Erasmus conceived the idea of collecting the most interesting proverbs and sayings, particularly those that had some application to contemporary life. These, under the pretext of explaining the meaning, would give him an excuse to add commentaries on current events. Thus the classical authors provided him with a shield.

The voyage which today lasts only a few hours took him a whole week, so that he had time to draw from his prodigious memory about eight hundred quotations. When he arrived in Paris, he wrote them out hastily, together with his commentaries, and gave them to a publisher. The latter, foreseeing the sensation they would cause, published the volume within a few weeks. It was the greatest publishing success — except that of the Bible — since the invention of printing. The book brought Erasmus only a few slim crowns, but it instantly made the author famous in all civilized countries. As the editions of the *Adages* were snatched up, they were continually reprinted — long after the death of Erasmus their vogue had not diminished — and the author continued to add to each edition new quotations accompanied by commentaries which grew bolder, more extended, and more explicit. Thus he made use of this admirable propaganda instrument in his peace campaign.

The two new adages he added to the edition of 1515. The commentaries by which he followed them have never since failed to attract attention. This is particularly true of his commentary on the phrase of Vegetius, in which he ridiculed and vehemently denounced the glorifiers of war, who, without themselves taking a risk, sent other people to fight, and used war to enrich themselves by the immolation and the desolation of the people.

In *Dulce Bellum Inexpertis* we find amplified the whole range of the grievances and arguments presented in his letter to the abbot of Saint-Bertin and to the Pope; but here the ideas are expressed with more sharpness, more firmness in the style (which is already approaching that of *Peace Protests!*) , and Erasmus returns to his idea of arbitration with more insistence. But above all he attacks the war profiteers, the conscienceless flatterers who, instead of urging peace, stirred up the kings and kept from court everyone who was opposed to war — "the honest subjects who are incapable of flattery." And, since any method was good when it was a question of enriching themselves on the blood of others, these criminals, under the pretext of defending and spreading the Christian religion, were preaching war against the Turks. Erasmus stripped the mask from these impudent fellows. "It is an offense against religion," he exclaimed indignantly, "to win the Turks by iron to the Christian religion. One should rather win them to Christianity by the example of a truly Christian life, by displaying a spirit of tolerance, by practicing scorn for the comforts of life, scorn for wealth."

These pages, commenting on the quotation of Vegetius, are among the finest and most inspired of Erasmus, and the problem of pacifism is posed in all its tragic amplitude. The vogue of the commentary on this adage was so extraordinary that, through the centuries, it has been translated more often and into more languages than *Peace Protests!* These translations are particularly numerous in English.

If, as has been rightly remarked, *Dulce Bellum Inexpertis* may be considered a preamble to *Peace Protests!*, his comments on *The Beetle and the Eagle* bear the same relationship to the *School for the Christian Prince*, which appeared the following year. But while in the latter work Erasmus attempted to paint the portrait of the ideal prince, in his commentaries on the Eagle he applied himself to portraying the bad prince, with such violence as no one, I believe, had ever used before in speaking of living kings. The adage in itself is insignificant and one is surprised at first by the length of the commentary which follows it. But as soon as one begins to read, one perceives that Erasmus used it only because it offered him a fine pretext for analyzing the reasons why the eagle is called "the king of birds," and why kings choose it as the symbol of royalty.

With feigned naïveté and biting irony, Erasmus is at first surprised that kings so willingly recognize themselves in this evil bird, "most powerful at doing evil, whose cruelty is never assuaged." Are those the characteristic traits of a king? In his simplicity Erasmus thinks otherwise. But kings should know best. The strangest thing is that they have chosen as their symbol, among all the various species of eagle, the one with the most hooked beak and the sharpest claws. In the humble opinion of the author, there should be no relationship between the "voracious bird, enemy of peace and repose, born for combat, rapine, and depredation," and kings, who are supposedly the fathers and benefactors of their people.

In the course of his analysis, Erasmus pretends to become more and more conscious of his own mistaken views. He reviews the misfortunes of the world, and soon perceives that kings must really be as they see themselves and that this horrible bird is actually their faithful portrait. No, they are worse! As he looks at them more closely, this portrait becomes flattery and deception. The kings try to mislead us when they claim to see themselves mirrored in the eagle. Compared with them, even this bird takes on a look of virtue. "Indeed," Erasmus goes on sarcastically, "the king of birds has only two eyes, one beak, ten claws, one single stomach. But in our 'eagles,' how many ears and eyes, how many claws and beaks, how many insatiable stomachs!" And our author, as with an artist's brush, begins to paint this rapacious bird. In spite of all the likenesses, he concludes, the eagle is far from resembling kings:

"To the strength and natural weapons of its body, the eagle adds the wiles of the spirit. When walking, it pulls back its claws so that their points will not be blunted and will have all their strength at the moment of attack. He attacks only an animal to which he believes himself superior in strength. . . . He hunts at his own hours and when there is no one in the fields. He does not devour his prey on the spot for fear of surprise; he carries it away to his aerie and does not return to the field until he has regained his strength. . . . If one thinks of the wiles, strategems, plots, and tricks with which bad princes arm themselves to despoil the people — fiscal laws, fines, false pretexts, hypocritical wars, denunciations, family alliances — one will agree that the eagle is truly unworthy to bear the name of king."

Hypocrisy is a sign of cowardice and the eagle is a coward just as are our great rulers. They have courage neither to tell the truth nor to hear it; and still less, to let others learn it. Thus they pursue with their hatred and their cruelty those who will not lower themselves to the level of flatterers and who abhor lies. The most effective adversaries of these tyrants are those who, lacking their weapons, still do not fear them. The weapons of these adversaries, scorned because of their physical weakness as much as they are feared, are wholly spiritual. These declared enemies of tyrants are not numerous but the more dangerous because, armed with their culture and their ideas, they continue to fight their oppressors even after death. These are the dreamers, the poets. Thus despots fear the free mind, and endeavor to keep their people in a state of ignorance, which however is only the reflection of their own. If that were not the case, they would aspire to elevate themselves to the height of the ideal ruler of Plato, by making their realm that dreamed-of republic where the king is a philosopher and the philosopher a king.

Erasmus continues his fine parallel:

"It is not surprising that this bellicose monster is at constant war with those poetic birds, the swans. What impresses us is that so warlike a monster is vanquished by them. The race of poets is just as unpopular with tyrants, whose consciences are uneasy, for the poets are an independent race and so garrulous that they sometimes prefer to be sent to hard labor rather than to be silent. They are so loquacious that if some subject annoys them, they transmit even beyond their tombs, to future generations, the secrets of kings. . . . Nor is the eagle a friend to the cranes, for the reason no doubt that the latter passionately love *democracy*, so hateful to tyrants. . . . And the eagle wages a merciless war on the night hawk, like the tyrants who hate nothing so much as those who, far from being satisfied to think like the herd, see clearly in the dark. . . ."

Erasmus is often forced to suggest rather than to state, to fall back upon irony and allusions. But the latter are so transparent that they amount almost to an appeal to overturn the existing political order — as he was soon to do openly in *Peace Protests!*, by raising before the eyes of rulers the specter of revolt if they continued to make war against the will of their peoples.

And yet, in spite of the language clothed in images and softened by the author's mocking smile, these sharp observations on the eagle and his human embodiment were never — to my knowledge — translated into a living tongue, at least not in Europe, before this century, where, until after the First World War, nearly every country was a monarchy. A translator or publisher would not have dared to make them available in a language accessible to all. Even in Latin, this text did not appear in its entirety except during the lifetime of the author, whose immense prestige prevented any pope or king from laying a hand on his writings. It was not until 1570, some decades after his death, that the most courageous passages began to disappear gradually even from the Latin editions, until finally they were more or less forgotten.

In 1516 appeared the *School of the Christian Prince* or *Institutio Principis Christiani,* Erasmus' most remarkable work on political morals. The author dedicated it to the royal heir, Charles of Austria, who, when the work left the presses, had just been proclaimed king.

While it was written for the use of a young prince, this work contains many pages which are of intrinsic pedagogical value in the education of any young man, especially in a period when a totalitarian plague leads astray the generous aspirations of a portion of our youth, when tyranny appears under so many masks and disguises, and when propaganda, carried to the extreme, perverts the most elementary notions of liberty, democracy, the popular will, and even peace.

After *Praise of Folly*, in which he had stung the tyrant with his sarcasm, after his pitiless parallel between the eagle and the king, Erasmus once more takes up the portrait of the bad prince. He proceeds like the painters of the Renaissance, opposing good and evil. Tracing the portraits of the tyrant king and the good king, he comes to the fine conclusion: A tyrant who rules by terror may, under the protection of guards armed to the teeth, display before his own people and other nations, his treasures, his luxury, his endless armaments. But in doing so, it is not his *power* that he reveals but his *strength*. For the powerful is only he who is just and good, who cherishes peace. A just prince does not need impressive spectacles to terrify his neighbors and his own subjects. A good prince needs neither guards nor police nor soldiers to make himself obeyed by his subjects and feared by his neighbors, because everyone knows, as he himself knows, that he is always surrounded by the affection and the gratitude of his people; because, obeying the will of his subjects, he is certain that in case of danger the whole nation will rally voluntarily behind him and fight at his side by their own will and with all their strength, whatever may be the reason for which the prince calls upon them. This fine definition of enslaving force and freeing power, this insistence upon the distinction between the two terms, is re-

markable: *Non potentia sed vis.* In its brevity, it still visual-
izes the tragic opposition between democracy and totali-
tarianism.

In the *Institutio* Erasmus introduced still another term
of great originality, which, at the end of nearly 450 years,
has not yet, alas, acquired citizenship rights among the
languages of civilized countries: the *art of peace.* The author
devotes a whole chapter to it, contrasting it with the *art of
war,* a too familiar term, even in the present day, in all
modern languages — the goal of military education.

The *art of peace* is nothing but the art of *avoiding* war;
it is more noble than the art of *making* it. It is more noble
because it is more difficult; and because it is more difficult
it is more glorious. It is more noble because it is proof of
the love that the head of the state has for his people; and
it is more glorious because it implies heroic self-mastery of
him who holds power: the resistance to intolerance, to blind
fanaticism, to tempting wealth. The greatest names in
history are not those distinguished by conquests or the found-
ing of empires at the expense of the independence of other
nations, by despoiling them and massacring them, as well
as by shedding the blood of their own people; but the names
of those who strengthened their states by peace, who contributed to the flourishing of the arts and sciences which
prosper in times of peace. It is true that history lists the
names of generals who were also great men, but they were
great only because of that quality in their lives which was
worthy of imitation and not because of their military exploits.
Seneca was right to call Alexander, Julius Caesar, Xerxes,
Darius, and other illustrious warriors, "furious brigands."

Peace and liberty are inseparable. The true greatness of
a chief of state consists in forgetfulness of himself for the
benefit of the state; he is a real master of his people only
to the extent that he is their servant. No law should be
promulgated, no measure taken, that is not the expression

of the will of the people. Laws are effective only to the extent that they are based on this popular will, instead of being the product of selfishness or the caprice of him who holds the power. Consequently, the king should be grateful to those who warn him against his own passions or his wrong judgment and punish those who flatter him. Indeed, he who flatters his prince when he deviates from these good principles should be punished as one punishes the poisoners of wells. To sum up: in spite of the right of succession, the legitimacy of power is only conditional. All power ceases to be legitimate when it becomes arbitrary.

Every chief of state should consider himself the trustee of the patrimony of the nation and as the father of his people toward whom he has obligations to fulfill. Consequently, he cannot dispose of this patrimony as though it were his private property, and he cannot use his people as an instrument to satisfy ambitions other than those of making them happy. It follows that one of his chief duties must be to watch over the members of the great family for which he is responsible lest some of them become too rich at the expense of their brothers; too great an inequality of fortune engenders social inequality, which leads to troubles inside the country, and ends by becoming a threat to outside neighbors which, in turn, leads to war.

Peace, to Erasmus, was an indivisible whole. Peace reigns only to the extent to which a country is governed to the satisfaction of all. And the more peace there is inside, the more it is engendered outside, being cause and effect at the same time. Cause and effect, however, are not obtained by a passive attitude. Peace is not a result of passivity. To create it, and derive all its benefits, requires a strong will and constant vigilance. For the art of peace is more difficult than the art of war and must, consequently, be learned with more application, as it takes far more knowledge to build than to destroy.

Everywhere there are military schools which teach the art of making war; but where are the schools where young men are taught the arts and tactics for winning, building, and strengthening peace? Their absence is one of the greatest contradictions in the life of nations which naturally aspire to peace. For, in spite of the frequency of wars, peace is the normal state of mankind. In the life of a nation war belongs to the domain of pathology, just as in the life of the individual, ill health is pathological. Health is still the normal state of man, in spite of the innumerable physical ills which overwhelm humanity. Since time immemorial men have learned to protect their health. Have we done as much for peace? A doctor, responsible for the well-being of the community, would be a charlatan if he were to ignore the dangers which threaten the health of those who rely on him and if he did not attempt to eliminate them. This charlatanism would become a crime in common law if a person offered to heal without first having learned how.

Should it not be the same with the man who is responsible for peace? How can he build and preserve it without knowing its complexity, without having studied it, without analyzing constantly its vulnerable points, without protecting it, without learning new methods of preserving it? Does a prince employ himself at these studies before taking power into his hands?

Formulated in 1516, these questions have not become obsolete today. Ruling princes and kings have nearly disappeared and, except in certain barbaric or half-barbaric countries, the power of those who still remain on their thrones has shrunk into insignificance. But Erasmus' questions have grown steadily in force and are more compelling now than ever before. In his times, regular military budgets were unknown and military expenses arbitrarily and secretly determined by autocrats. Free modern states have regular and democratically approved military budgets. Now, if we translate the words of Erasmus in up-to-date terms — keeping in mind that, whatever his all-out pacifism, he did not deny to peaceful nations (as we will see in analyzing *Peace Protests!*) the right to protect themselves against unprovoked aggressions — we might enlarge on his questions:

Is there a single nation which, however free and peace-minded, has in any way parallel with its *military budget,* designed for defensive purposes, a regular *peace budget,* intended to teach the "art of peace" inside and outside its own country? Yet such a requirement would be the modern expression of what Erasmus so desperately tried to impress upon governments. In fact, Erasmus' thought, whatever its shape, was the very same which Senator Brien McMahon of Connecticut (who, being Chairman of the Joint Committee on Atomic Energy, is the highest Congressional authority in this field) — echoing the proposal of Mr. Bernard Baruch to the Assembly of the United Nations in 1946, for worldwide control of atomic energy — expressed in his now historic speech, delivered on the floor of the United States Senate on February 2, 1950. If a peace budget, which the Senator demanded, had allowed this speech to be adequately disseminated, and thus made known in the most remote corners of the globe the genuine aspirations of the people and government of the United States, it would have done more to teach misinformed and enslaved peoples liberty and to foster peace than our expensive military program and the "Whisper of America" — as McMahon ironically called the "Voice of America" — have been able to achieve. Rightly and with much wisdom the Senator pointed out that the existence of such a peace budget would soon prove more practical, more effective in averting war and in strengthening the United Nations, than the most ruinous military budgets and the deadliest weapons.

Indeed, "the human voice is mightier than a hundred trumpets." This sentence taken from John Calvin can be read, engraved, on one of the walls of the Swiss city of Geneva. Calvin, younger contemporary of Erasmus, said it at a time when people still believed that Jericho fortresses could be crumbled by the mere sounds of a blessed trumpet. But the modern sense of what the Geneva Reformer said remains as true today as its former meaning was true to the contemporaries of Erasmus. If, thanks to a peace budget, the voice of liberty and peace were indefatigably and generously diffused throughout the world, it could still work miracles and prove more powerful in crumbling fortresses, in achieving peace, and in implanting freedom everywhere, than hundreds and even thousands, not of trumpets but of atom and hydrogen bombs. In expressing this belief, Senator McMahon caused America on that occasion to speak the language of the great world citizen Erasmus. Nonetheless, the humanist's question still remains open.

Furthermore and always translating the questions of Erasmus in up-to-date terms: How many of our statesmen devote themselves to the subject of peace before seeking public office? The man of political ambition who has been placed in a position to govern, but who has not first studied peace, is not worthy of his office. For it is not enough to learn this art after one has taken office. It is irresponsible to learn it at the cost of disaster, discovering after ruinous experiences that war does not pay. One must foresee these horrors and know how to avert them.

Erasmus insists that the man who holds power and on whom the fate of his people depends cannot be permitted to acquire this wisdom only at the end of his life — if he ever does! — when he must say to himself remorsefully: Immortal God, at the cost of how many universal sorrows hast Thou taught me this truth!

The building of peace requires the highest moral qualities, one being absolutely essential: wholehearted sincerity. Any international treaty made with reservations and without the desire to establish permanent peace is a crime and should be regarded as a conspiracy against the public welfare. Any treaty signed in good faith is a contribution to outlawing war. Moreover, good faith and sincere friendship are safer guaranties of peace than the most elaborate treaties. Erasmus is surprised that well-meaning people need so many written agreements, and he especially distrusts those which have a number of clauses. In his chapter on treaties he writes:

"In signing treaties, as in everything else, the good prince must be guided by no thought but of what is advantageous to his people. In the opposite case . . . a treaty is only a conspiracy. . . . When an affair is regulated by so many written agreements, it is a proof that the thing is not done in good faith. Indeed, we often see that many litigious acts result from these very agreements which were drawn up for the sole purpose of preventing any possibility of litigation. When there is good faith and the affair is handled by honest persons, there is no reason for so many treaties so painfully worked out. . . . But in the hands of stupid and wicked rulers, these very same treaties, signed to prevent any return of war, become the causes of war, because one of the contracting parties makes use of them in order to complain, that, among their innumerable articles, such and such clause was violated.

"Ordinarily a treaty was drawn up to put an end to wars; but at the present time any agreement is called a treaty which serves as a point of departure for a new war. In reality, all these alliances are nothing but preparations for war."

There are lofty chapters in *Institutio Principis Christiani*, pages of exquisite beauty that can be read over and over. Contemporary readers seized upon the work like an unknown and fascinating jewel, from which they could not turn away their eyes. We find echoes of that excitement not only in the incessant flood of editions, but in the written testimony that has come down to our own days. I will mention only that of Thomas Elyot, an English author, today largely forgotten but in his own time greatly appreciated as a writer and perspicacious and enthusiastic commentator on the works of Erasmus. In his *Book of the Governor*, which appeared in 1531, some fifteen years after the publication of the *Institutio,* Elyot observed that this work was still the most popular, most widely read and quoted literary production of the period; probably, he added, as popular as the works of Homer had been with such remarkable men of Antiquity as Xenophon or Alexander the Great.

The book is crammed full of ideas which impress us as much by their originality as by their courage. And while it has not altogether escaped the ravages of time, this work still glows with literary beauty. For today's reader it is suggestive on more than one point, applying as well to the principles of modern government as to those of yesterday. And its title and subject involuntarily evoke another celebrated work, dating almost from the same year as that of Erasmus, which is its very antithesis: *The Prince* by Niccolò Machiavelli.

To read these two works together, even superficially, is to bring out all the originality and all the courage of Erasmus. For his political ideals were not those of his time. The spokesman for the ethics practised by the Renaissance was Machiavelli, whose moral code — or that of the princes which he astutely divulged — is still, in some countries, that of our own day. The four and a half centuries which have passed since Erasmus formulated his precepts have not been long enough to make them timely. One can therefore imagine the current against which the little monk struggled, virtually alone. For while he had many friends and a host of admirers who thought as he did, no one dared to express himself as openly or as loudly as he, not even the courageous Thomas More in his charming reverie, *Utopia*.

The overwhelming majority of the intellectuals of the Renaissance, humanist as they were, conceived of the administration of the state as Machiavelli did, especially in domestic policies. Contemptuous of the people, they had no interest in their fate. Erasmus, while equally contemptuous because of their illiteracy, had however an immense pity for the little people and an ardent desire to raise them out of their ignorance and poverty, for which he held the ruling class and its flatterers responsible.

While Erasmus was considered in his own time, and afterwards, as the greatest writer and moralist of the Renaissance, he represented only its ideal aspect. The best representation of its practical aspect was and remains the author of *The Prince*. Machiavelli was flesh of its flesh while Erasmus was its conscience. Erasmus criticized the political and religious morals and contrasted them with his concepts of a state ethics and a church ideal, while Machiavelli raised the existing immorality to dogma. Erasmus drew the portrait of the prince as he should be, Machiavelli painted him as he was. Erasmus thought of the well-being of humanity, Machiavelli sacrificed them to the well-being of rulers. Erasmus preached to the prince the indispensable virtues of making himself loved by the people and safeguarding peace, but Machiavelli recommended this:

"It is not only unnecessary to have all these virtues, but it is prejudicial to have them and to practice them all the time. On the other hand, it is useful to *seem* to have them. A prince must appear merciful, loyal, religious, humane, but, if necessary, he must know how to be the opposite. . . . His soul must be able to switch back as circumstances and fortune command. . . . He must be careful never to speak a word that will betray the qualities indicated above, so that he may appear to those who see and hear him all goodness, all humanity, all good faith, all integrity, all religion. *This last quality is the one whose appearance matters the most.* . . . Thus everyone sees the prince as he appears to be; few understand what he is. And this small minority dares not stand against the opinion of the majority which has the majesty of the State behind it. . . . The minority only enters the game when the multitude does not know where to turn. . . ." (*Il Principe,* Chap. XVIII) .

Whereas Erasmus set as the essential condition of the right to govern a continual study of the art of peace, as well as absolute sincerity, Machiavelli made basic principles of perjury and the tireless study of the art of war. "It is praiseworthy for a prince to keep his word," dogmatized this author, "but a prince neither can nor should keep it when his faith works against him and the reasons for his promise no longer exist. . . . *Princes should make the art of war their only study and their only occupation*: that, properly speaking, is the science of those who govern . . ." (*Del Arte della Guerra*) .

One could continue the parallels between these two works from the first page to the last, each a refutation of the other. It is remarkable that *Institutio Principis Christiani* and *Il Principe* were composed almost simultaneously without either author's even suspecting it. For reasons that may never be cleared up, the famous work of Machiavelli was not published until fifteen years after that of Erasmus— four years after the death of its author. Doubtless Erasmus never read it, as he too died five years after the publication of *Il Principe*. In any case, we do not find the slightest mention of it either in his letters or in his works.

7.

The Art of Peace

SPEAKING OF PASCAL, whom he admired while rejecting certain phases of his spiritualism, Voltaire said that it is the privilege of real genius to be mistaken with impunity. He forgot another such privilege: to repeat oneself without being a bore. That was Erasmus' prerogative. He deliberately repeated himself like those great artists who, in infinite variations, return to the same central motif. For the work of Erasmus, whatever the wealth of its ideas may be, impresses us perhaps by the variety of these less than by the ingenious variations on his fundamental ideas, which, like leitmotifs, emerge in each of his writings. Indeed, what strikes the attentive reader when he has closed the book and freed himself from the immediate charm of the author, is not the continual play of new thoughts, but fresh appearances of the same ones, the impetuous ardor with which he throws new light upon them. By this method Erasmus achieves the most convincing effects. By repeating his ideas, he illuminates them each time more vividly, with an ever sharper focus, like a face that is reproduced from various aspects until one sees it in its entirety as well as in its smallest details.

From this point of view, *Peace Protests!* is a summing-up. All Erasmus' ideas on peace are gathered together; but each of them has become more concrete, reduced to its simplest terms.

In its construction, *Peace Protests!* differs from the other works of Erasmus, where the author's ideas are linked together with the logic of nature itself, and where he does not abandon one until he has exhausted its possibilities. Here, on the other hand, although he reveals the same implacable logic, he slows or accelerates the development, occasionally drops one idea for another as though interrupting himself, returns to it, leaves it, retraces his steps, but each time more forcefully, until his thought rings out in the most definite terms. There is no doubt that these leaps and returns of the consummate stylist and strategist were intentional. Far from being a weakness, they rather demonstrate a new strategy, chosen to meet his needs. In this work, Erasmus intended to wage a decisive battle, after having carefully prepared the ground. What he desired was no longer merely to condemn war or make recommendations for peace; but to accomplish concrete results, to make himself heard, to convince, to force action not only upon his habitual readers and admirers, who, like himself, were observers or helpless actors in the drama, but upon the powerful, who were the authors and stage managers of the play. The method which he chose for this purpose was doubtless the one most likely to attract them and prevent them from closing the book until they had heard to the very end the denunciatory diatribe of Peace speaking in person.

Oddly enough, while Erasmus was the best-informed man on the events of his time, and while his works and letters constitute even today one of our most complete and valuable sources on them, some of his commentators have claimed naïvely that when he wrote *Peace Protests!* he was ill-informed on what was going on in the various European courts. Why? Because, after having pilloried the princes and their advisers, among whom the dignitaries of the Church of Rome occupied the place of honor, Erasmus distributed praises to the three most powerful autocrats in Christendom as well as to the Pope, as though to underline the fact that his grave accusations were not addressed to them. Other critics went so far as to claim that the old fox, the keen psychologist, was deceived about the true state of affairs by the statesmen involved — for instance, Chancellor Sauvage — who encouraged him to write this work for the sole purpose of concealing, behind the moral authority of Erasmus, the sinister designs of their masters.

This allegation simply will not stand up. Literally, it is true that Erasmus, as counselor of state to Charles V, was the subordinate of Chancellor Sauvage. It is even true that the chancellor wanted him to write a book on peace, favorable to the plans of his government. But as Erasmus accepted his post only as an honorary title and after long hesitation — only, that is, after he was assured that he was to bear the title and receive the salary without having to devote the slightest scrap of his time or his liberty to it — it was he who had the moral authority to suggest his ideas to the chancellor rather than the latter daring to impose his own.

So far as the flattery at the end of *Peace Protests!* is concerned, I have already had occasion to indicate what Erasmus himself thought of it and of the credence he expected to be attached to it. In this case, in particular, by permitting Peace to flatter certain princes, Erasmus made them appear even more ridiculous than he had showed them to be evil: he spat out his scorn, only to add that he was not spitting in their faces. That was the trick of a good comedian rather than a man who had been misled.

Henry VIII and Maximilian I, as no contemporary reader could help recalling, were among those responsible for the recent wars; and Prince Charles and his grandfather Maximilian came first to mind when Erasmus condemned royal marriages as sources of war and oppression. For Maximilian I, that perennial suitor, was always getting married, collecting the inheritance of his dead wives, remarrying or marrying off some member of his family for the purpose of enlarging his Empire. He began by betrothing his grandson, the future

Charles V, when the latter was only one year old! As some of his fiancées, or their fathers, changed their mind in time and some territorial promises were contested, the Emperor waged war to attempt to seize the vanished dowries by force. The whole world knew it, and no one could be mistaken as to whom Erasmus was indicting.

One must really be devoid of all sense of the comic not to perceive that by praising Maximilian by name at the conclusion of his violent arraignment, Erasmus abandoned him to more pitiless public contempt than when he attacked without calling him by name. True, his praise of the two younger kings was sincere, because he was still justified in having illusions in regard both to Francis I and Charles V. But when he perceived that his hopes were unfounded, Erasmus did not hesitate to say so, as he did about Pope Leo X. On the whole, he expressed himself in *Peace Protests!* on kings, popes, cardinals, bishops, theologians, monks, lawyers— often synonymous with diplomats — and armies, in such a fashion that the slight approving smile given to a few poten- tates — after having dragged in the mud the whole ruling class of Europe — was really cheap at the price so long as he succeeded in making himself heard in every land in Christendom.

Peace Protests! is a masterpiece without any counterpart in the pacifist literature of the world. And among the works of Erasmus, it is perhaps the only one which has not suf- fered from the ravages of time, remaining as fresh as at the moment of its publication in 1517. As I have already pointed out, if one were merely to replace the princes by certain less pompous but equally powerful individuals in our own century; the royal marriages by the economic politics of the international trusts; other terms by modern equivalents of a social, economic, or political order, even the examples by which the author illustrates the abuses of his own time against peace would become, in some countries at least, those of our own century — not to mention his ideas on the abolition of war and the organization of permanent peace whose intrinsic value remains unchanged, even greater in 1950 than in 1517.

Yet it is both strange and disturbing that, in the hundreds of works which have appeared on Erasmus over the centuries, his critics and his interpreters have rarely mentioned this masterpiece, and, when they have done so, devoted only a few words or lines to it. Is this because of the brevity of the text or rather because the subject itself mattered so little that our scholars, thinkers, and writers preferred the so-called theological ideas of Erasmus — I mean those that were purely moral and religious?

This question suggests another: Has Erasmus really been understood? Naturally, he dealt with theological problems, like most of the writers of his time. But by concentrating their interest entirely on his theological ideas, have not most of his interpreters given a wrong emphasis to Erasmus and his work? At the risk of shocking some of his fervent admirers, as well as his ardent haters, I would even say that theology—"that frigid, quarrelsome old lady, swollen to such a point of vanity that she must be deflated to bring her back to her source," as Erasmus characterized her — was not his final goal, but a means that was admirably effective in his day. His real goal was the education of humanity for the attainment of perpetual peace and the brotherhood of man. Spiritual and material peace — that was the goal of all that Erasmus wrote and thought. We pervert the inheritance he left us when we insist on centering the thought and activity of Erasmus around any pivot but Peace — Peace in all its aspects, using the Church and lay institutions as means.

It follows that by not mentioning *Peace Protests!*, by not pausing long before his pacifist ideas, by failing to see in them the shining reflection of all his spiritual and humanitarian aspirations as well as the ways for realizing his objectives, we misunderstand the true essence of his ideals and his struggle, we strip from his personality and his work their most original, most characteristic, and perhaps most enduring element. To cite only one example, I have before me one of the most recent biographies of Erasmus (*Erasmus von Rotterdam,* by K. A. Meissinger, Zurich, 1942). I do not single it out because of its outstanding merits, although, crammed with knowledge and written in German, it bears the stamp of an unquestionably humanistic mind, which probably explains why the work appeared during the war in Switzerland rather than in Germany. And yet it does not even mention *Peace Protests!* And that at a time when the sanguinary circumstances should have recalled the existence and importance of such a work to the most forgetful among the students of the life and writings of Erasmus.

The fact is that only since the beginning of this century, especially since the First World War, have some historians of Erasmus begun to realize the place this little book occupies in the immense work of its author. We must, however, give credit to the instinctive homage of the average reader, who for a long time grasped the value of this work infinitely better than the scholars and the biographers. For *Peace Protests!* had an immense vogue during the lifetime of its author as well as during the centuries that have passed since his death.

In the literary world, those who in the last decades have best revealed its value are in my opinion the following authors: P. S. Allen, an Englishman, in his monumental edition of Erasmus' letters, already mentioned, and in his *Age of Erasmus* (Oxford, 1914). His wife, Mrs. P. S. Allen, in *Erasmus on Peace,* published on the occasion of the four hundredth anniversary of Erasmus' death (in *Voordrachten gehouden ter herdenking van den stefdag van Erasmus op 10 en 11 Juli 1936 te Rotterdam,* The Hague, 1936). Madame

Elise Constantinescu Bagdat, in her doctor's dissertation in French, *La "Querela Pacis" d'Erasme* (Paris, 1924). The German, T. Thürlemann, in his scholarly work *Erasmus von Rotterdam und Joannes Ludovicus Vives als Pazifisten* (Freiburg, 1932). The Austrian, Stefan Zweig, that world citizen and ardent pacifist, who, having devoted most of his strength to peace, lost faith in its realization, and despairing of the future, preferred to be engulfed by the storm during the Second World War; his work, *Triumph und Tragik des Erasmus von Rotterdam* (Vienna, 1935), without exhausting the subject and without being a work of scholarship, to which its author never pretended, is valuable chiefly because of its emphasis on the pacifist nature of Erasmus. The American scholar Lester K. Born, in the introduction to his translation of *Institutio Principis Christiani* (Columbia University Press, 1936). Finally, A. Renaudet, professor at the Sorbonne in Paris, an old Erasmus student and author of several important works on him. In *Etudes Erasmiennes* (1521-1529) (Paris, 1939), although dealing with a period subsequent to the publication of *Querela Pacis*, Renaudet gives one of the finest analyses ever made of the political and pacifist ideas of the author of *Peace Protests!*

The dissertation of Madame Constantinescu Bagdat, devoted exclusively to *Querela Pacis*, is distinguished particularly by its scientific material, its bibliography, its detailed analysis of the ideas of Erasmus on peace, and the accumulation of information, facts and dates with which it is crammed. However, this scholarly work contains a few factual errors as well as gaps which are explained doubtless by the fact that its author is familiar with the Erasmian literature chiefly in French and German. Thus she indicates as publication date of the first English translation of this work by Thomas Paynell, under the title of *The Complaint of Peace*, the year 1802 — whereas it was 1559, twenty-three years after the death of Erasmus. The works on Erasmus written by American scholars are not mentioned, nor are the editions of *Peace Protests!* which have appeared at various times in this country, particularly the edition of 1813 — published doubtless as a protest against the war between England and the United States. (It is true that the title under which this work appeared in New York in 1813 might have failed to attract the attention of the author of the scholarly dissertation: *The Plea of Reason, Religion and Humanity against War* by Erasmus.)

These reprints have become, in a way, a pacifist tradition throughout civilized countries. The vogue of *Peace Protests!* has revived whenever war has struck at the people. We have just seen that it was circulated in the United States at the time of the War of 1812. It appeared again during the First World War; and shortly after the Second World War there was published in New York a fine edition in facsimile of the translation by Thomas Paynell, *The Complaint of Peace* by Erasmus, with a scholarly introduction by William James Hirten (Scholars' Facsimiles & Reprints, New York, 1946). But among all these reprints, there was not *one* new translation. For four centuries, people have been satisfied to reproduce that of Paynell, sometimes modernizing it. I will return to this question in my Translator's Introduction on page 125.

This manifesto has been used as a weapon not only by pacifists and protesters against war but also by warring governments. Official propaganda has transformed this indictment of war into a nationalistic and chauvinistic weapon by disseminating, *urbi et orbi,* the good that Erasmus, uncompromising pacifist, had said of their respective countries, and taking no account of what he had said of their adversaries. Thus, in 1802, during the war between England and Napoleon, the edition that appeared in London — still the translation of Thomas Paynell, who had published it more than three centuries before, perhaps at the risk of his life! — omitted the lavish praise Erasmus had given France; while the Napoleonic government in France probably exploited against England the admiration which the great pacifist felt for its enemy, leaving out the praise he had bestowed on the country of Thomas More. No one is safe from the revolting abuses of this kind of propaganda. During the Second World War we saw how the Hitler propaganda machine seized upon all pacifist criticisms of their own governments as expressing approval of the odious Nazi regime or as a sign of solidarity with the hideous manslaughter which these monsters were inflicting on mankind.

This procedure, one sees, is not the exclusive privilege of our own century — although the latter has far richer means than any which preceded it of justifying the popular German verse:

Kommt ein Krieg ins Land,
Gibt es Luegen wie Sand

("When a nation is at war, there are as many lies as sand.")

Erasmus, in his pacifist manifesto, had already denounced vehemently the "poisonous propaganda" of warlike governments, warning that one must guard against it even before war breaks out. For war cannot be fought without preparing minds in advance. But, in spite of all the warnings repeated for centuries, we are still far from being immune to this poison. Aside from the hatred of the foreigner that it inculcates, this propaganda dishonors and renders contemptible every citizen whose conscience revolts against wholesale massacre. "And here," Peace goes on, "is where things stand at present. Nothing is more imprudent or more unrighteous than to protest against war, than to praise what Jesus, with his own mouth, praised above all things. Thus, any man who urges peace (that is to say, the most salutary thing), any man who wants to turn his country away from war (which is the worst thing), is regarded as a bad patriot who reveals little interest in the happiness of his people."

According to Erasmus, love for one's people and true

patriotism are revealed best not by advocating but by opposing war. For, aside from the moral and material ruin that it
causes, war is incapable, as history proves, of solving the
problems that overwhelm humanity. On the contrary, instead of diminishing their number, it always adds more. Instead of bringing us nearer to peace, therefore, war drives it
each time farther away. For war cannot put an end to war;
each one engenders others, and so on to the end — like the
mythological hydra heads. "Let anyone tell me," demands
Peace, "what war, even the shortest, has not made way for
a new war that was infinitely longer? . . . Which, at last, is
the one that, not cruel in the beginning, has not become
a monstrously bloody war when this evil, by being prolonged,
ended by exhausting the nerves of the people to the point
of exasperation?"

It follows that those who judge the degree of a man's devotion to his country or his civic virtues by his promptness
to accept war are either blind to what war really means —
in which case it is our duty to open their eyes — or hypocrites
from whom true patriots should strip the mask. For we are
concerned here with a fallacy, a reversal of the facts. "They
complain," Peace points out, "of being forced, in spite of
themselves, into war. Let that mask be stripped from them!
Let us deny this false pretext!" War is not a necessity, because there are, when used in time, means of avoiding it; nor
does it promote virtue in those who take part in it. For war
is the school of crime. War is a source not of virtues but of
the greatest vices. Without it, without the material damage
that it causes, without the relaxation of morals which it engenders, human vices would never take on such monstrous
proportions. On the other hand, the man who fights for the
preservation of peace contributes to the material and moral
preservation of his national patrimony, as well as to the
progress and well being of his people: "If there is anything
really great," says Peace, "it is to see a country living in

abundance, flourishing in all the arts, with cities solidly built, and well-cultivated fields, enjoying liberal and just laws, cultivating useful sciences, and having irreproachable habits. And now . . . if you have ever seen ruined cities, villages reduced to ashes, burned churches, devastated fields, and if this spectacle seems to you as desolate as it is in reality, tell yourself that that is the work of war . . . If you have a horror of brigandage, what is war but brigandage on a gigantic scale? If you abominate parricide, it is in war that it is learned . . . War is the scourge of states, the tomb of justice . . . War encourages murder, opprobium, adultery, incest." And Erasmus proceeds to a rapid analysis of the reasons invoked in favor of war, demolishing them one by one in ringing phrases which, through their clarity and brevity, resound like a regular barrage.

It is strange that anthologies of wisdom, which have been published in recent years more frequently than ever before, never include aphorisms of Erasmus expressing the wisdom of Peace. Perhaps I may encourage someone to do so if I reproduce here some specimens taken from *Peace Protests!*:

Peace, by means of commercial exchange, makes all things common.

A state, we know, disintegrates when the evil have too much authority. In time of war, the evil reign as masters.

There is no victory which does not do evil to men, for there is none which is not stained with human blood.

You will reply, I know, that it is not right for a lofty spirit not to avenge himself for injuries. No! There is no more certain indication of a debased soul than the fact of avenging himself.

One cannot block the enemy at his frontiers without being forced at the same time to isolate his own country from many other states.

It would have cost far less to build new cities than to demolish with your war machines existing cities.

Lasting peace resides not . . . in the treaties . . . which usually lead to wars. It is necessary to clean out *the very source* from which the evil comes. [It is interesting to compare the terminology of Erasmus with that of our own day; Pandit Nehru, in his speech delivered at Columbia University on October 17, 1949, said: "If we seek to ensure peace, we must attack *the root causes of war* and not merely the symptoms."]

It is a magnificent thing to disregard self-interest and to measure everything by the common interest.

The distance from our country to another separates bodies and not souls.

Almost all the causes of war spring from motives that have nothing to do with the common good.

Most of the people detest war and desire peace. A small number, whose accursed happiness always depends upon the misfortune of the common people, want war. Must their inhumanity outweigh the will of so many good people?

Wars lead to wars. Vengeance attracts vengeance. Indulgence creates indulgence. Good will invites to good will. Thus those who yield even a small part of their rights will enjoy the greatest happiness.

Peace rests largely in the fact of desiring it with all the force of our soul.

How slight and futile are the real causes of the great disasters which afflict humanity!

Jesus called himself a shepherd, and he called his disciples his sheep; but what must the wolves do if the sheep destroy each other?

From what hell does the demon come who succeeds in injecting the poison into the hearts of Christians? . . . They are wild beasts, rather than men, noble only to the extent that tyranny can make them noble. They have never united except to do evil.

He who wishes for health desires an excellent thing. But the man who ardently asks for peace asks at the same time for the most perfect happiness.

"There are cases where *we must buy peace*." It is in *Peace Protests!* that Erasmus so bluntly formulates, for the first time in his writings, this method of avoiding war. Should one evoke national honor, in rejecting certain means of keeping peace, it would only be a pretext, for the honor of a nation consists first in safeguarding peace and not spilling blood. However, it would be false to conclude that Erasmus, in all cases, preached passivity in the face of aggression. Although he abhorred violence, he was *not* an advocate of unconditional non-resistance. Obviously, in condemning all wars of aggression or imperialism, Erasmus did not tolerate defensive war, either, so long as it could be avoided even by "buying" peace. In his opinion, no ransom was too high in case of success. But if, in spite of the exorbitant price that a nation would be ready to pay for peace, it could not buy off the aggressor, then the pacifists should resist as one resists murderers who enter our houses to kill our wives and children.

In any case, whatever its character, no war should be undertaken without the unanimous approval of the nation: "War, which is the most dangerous thing there is, should not be undertaken except with the consent of the entire nation." Otherwise, the peoples have the right to revolt against their leaders and to drive them out of power. (For the moral reasons and the legality of driving princes out of power, and even expelling them from their countries, as well as the justification of such a reaction by the people, in case their sovereigns should act against the popular will, see Note 5, page 186.) Expressed in unequivocal form, while addressing the mightiest potentates of his time, this thought went beyond the

audacity to which Erasmus had accustomed us: it was equivalent to denying openly the divine rights of princes, inalien-
able by men. And yet it was only a logical conclusion to
what he had already said in *Institutio Principis Christiani*.

The idea that the sovereignty of the popular will surpasses everything else and should serve as the law which the
princes must obey, had been formulated long before Erasmus.
Even Aristotle dealt with it. Nevertheless — and in spite of
Dante, whose opinion on that subject was closely related to
that of Erasmus — he was the first to draw such *radical* conclusions from it.

Some historians have compared his attitude with that of
Thomas Aquinas which, they believe, was similar. But this
comparison does not sustain analysis. There is a major difference between the position of the "angelic doctor," against
which Dante had already protested, and that of the author
of *Peace Protests!* Thomas Aquinas *did* demand that the
will of the people be respected by the prince; but, convinced
of the divine right of kings and putting all his confidence in
the direct intervention of God in case they should abuse this
right, the author of *Summa Theologica* did *not* admit that
the subjects themselves could maintain their right by direct
action; whereas Erasmus was not afraid to warn princes
against what would await them if they plunged their country
into war without the prior consent of those whose well-being
was confided to them.

From the time of his letter to the abbot of Saint-Bertin,
Erasmus constantly demanded the setting up of a court of
international arbitration. He takes up this idea more forcefully in *Peace Protests!*, without however drawing all the logical conclusions which a reader of our day might expect.
Erasmus clearly foresees the case in which one of the parties
in litigation would not submit to the decision of a court of
arbitration; but he does not say how this problem should
be solved. Is it the threatened state which must force its

adversary to submit to the will of the arbitrator? Then what authority would the court of arbitration have? — for if the one desiring war were the stronger, it could crush the weaker one that ordered it to respect international law. A court invested with the right of pronouncing judgment must be able to impose it without leaving that task to the plaintiff, for the purpose of such an institution is to make *all war* lawless.

Thus there is a gap in the proposal of Erasmus. No doubt he postponed the complete development for a later work to be devoted to international arbitration, which he did not have time to write. Indeed, if events had not forced him to interrupt his peace offensive, in order to bring all his efforts to bear on another battlefield, it is logical that Erasmus would finally have denied any state the right to bear arms, even for the purpose of self-defense against an aggressor who refused to accept the judgment of an International Court. He might have proposed that this task be confided to a permanent international police force, whose duty would be to keep peace in every state. And, to this end, he would, doubtless, have demanded general disarmament.

Although Erasmus did not inform us of all the conclusions which his project of arbitration might have suggested to him, he did reach a conclusion of a totally different nature which, even if undeveloped, is of major importance. Since love of country is so profoundly rooted that men are ready, in the defense of their fellow-citizens, to sacrifice their lives, why not make a greater virtue of extending this love to all humanity — that is, make all countries part of a single whole, all states united in a universal federation of states? *"If the name of country is of such nature as to create bonds between those who have a common country, why,"* suggests Peace, *"do not men resolve that the universe should become the country of all?"*

In making this proposal, Erasmus did not limit such a state to the Christian world alone, but to all men — the title of *man* being in his eyes superior to that of *Christian,* because it was more universal. Whatever the boldness of making such a deduction from Erasmus' proposal, I nevertheless do not believe I am mistaken in interpreting his thought in this sense. Indeed, almost at the end of his work, the author, through the mouth of Peace, makes the following plea: "It is time to amend your ways. If the shedding of *Christian* blood seems to you of little importance, then more than enough *human* blood has flowed, so that this frenzy of exterminating each other should come to an end. You have sacrificed enough to the infernal furies." And as though to stress the moral superiority of human brotherhood, without distinction of race or religion, over all other bonds, Peace concludes: *"The most sublime thing is to deserve well of the human race."*

No author before Erasmus had formulated the idea of a pan-human state as concretely as he did. It was so novel that, even in our times, after two world wars in three decades, it is still far from having become an axiom for all the world. I say "as concretely," for, before him, other thinkers had not failed to suggest something similar, limiting it expressly to the Christian world. Erasmus, loathing the Middle Ages, does not mention them, as though he had never heard of them. It is probable that, with his distaste for what was medieval, he had not even read its political or moral treatises, except those of the Church Fathers. But, whatever the reason for his silence, Erasmus owed nothing to his scholastic predecessors, and his originality is complete.

This originality results not from the novelty of what a genius has said, but from the new way in which he has said it, from the grouping of ideas which are his own. For instance, the statement has often been made that many of the aphorisms of Jesus and almost all the phrases of the Lord's Prayer are to be found in the Jewish wise men who preceded him and who largely inspired him. Or that, in particular, he borrowed from Hillel, that gentle sage who

died in the year 4 A.D., certain of whose sentences had become
in his lifetime so proverbial that Jews used them in their
daily speech. And so did Jesus. But the most sublime phrases,
the most lofty thoughts, the most profound proverbs and
parables do not in themselves make a whole work, just as the
most beautiful diamonds do not make a crown. It is he who
forms them into a whole, who gives them an individual existence, who makes the form and imposes his personality on it,
who lends them an originality that reflects his own. And that
is why the teachings of Jesus bear the name not of Hillelism
but of Christianity. One might say as much for what I would
call the pacifist doctrine of Erasmus.

The fact is that those who had preceded Erasmus along
this same road only *appeared* to speak of the same thing or
only alluded to something, which was no more than a neb-
ulous dream. Dante, for example, exiled from his native
Florence, was so unhappy that he desired a universal monarchy from which it would be impossible to banish anyone
and which would make no more wars; but this was only the
dream of a great poet who hated war and suffered from the
unjust manner in which his ungrateful country had treated
him. And so with the federalist or universalist aspirations of
some moralists of the Middle Ages. The only serious project
that preceded the period of Erasmus, a project indeed more
thoroughly elaborated than that which the author of *Peace
Protests!* offered, was that of a great French jurist, Pierre
Dubois, dating from the beginning of the fourteenth century.
Dubois developed a real charter for a world state — or, rather,
a Christian state. This project had only one fault, but a
major one, which would have sufficed for Erasmus to reject
it if he had known of it: that of serving the imperialist ambitions of a single country. Its author proposed that at the
head of this world state should be placed the "most Christian
king" of France, who would thus become sovereign and arbi-
ter of Christendom, with Paris no doubt as its capital.

The idea Erasmus was building of a pan-human community was of a totally different stamp and spirit. His federated
universal state was to embrace the human race, to unite all
peoples as equals, without anyone, great or small, sacrificing
anything for the profit of another and without any nation
emerging enlarged at the expense of other nations. Basically,
this was the same idea that Woodrow Wilson conceived in
1916, which, after many mutilations and concessions, emerged
as the impotent League of Nations. It was also the idea that
presided over the creation of the United Nations—whose final
goal will be attained only on the day when the United States
of the World will emerge and this organization will become
its government. So if ever this universal state is realized, its
spiritual paternity, in part at least, must be attributed to
Erasmus.

Peace Protests!, which marks the climax of Erasmus' offensive for universal peace, became unexpectedly its final point.
It is true that thirteen years later, in 1530, he published another little work in which he dismissed all the arguments
advanced in favor of a war against the Turks; now he disavowed the military projects of Charles V, his sovereign, protector and admirer. But this publication was only a cry
of indignation, the familiar cry that resounded throughout
Erasmus' life in most of his unpolitical works, not a part of
a constructive plan, and not of the same importance as his
other political writings on peace. In launching his manifesto
in 1517, Erasmus himself could not have foreseen that he
would be brought to a halt in the midst of his all-out attack,
carefully prepared for years.

About the time of *Peace Protests!*, Martin Luther appeared
on the horizon. Erasmus joyously welcomed his entry on the
scene. But the situation soon took a violent turn and Erasmus hastened to devote most of his energy to spiritual peace
— in his mind the fundamental prelude to material peace.

Nevertheless, while no longer devoting himself to special works of an outspoken political character, he continued to protest on every occasion against those who waged war, and to denounce vehemently the connivance of the clergy with the bloodshedding princes whom, he said, the priests and the monks encouraged in their criminal enterprises.

Indeed, nothing is more characteristic of this attitude of Erasmus in the fateful years which succeeded the publication of *Peace Protests!* than some of his unpolitical works. Take, for instance, *Charon,* that sparkling dialogue between Alastor, the avenging god of the Greeks, and Charon, the ferryman of the dead in the realm of shadows. (I stop before *Charon* in preference to other works of the period, because of the year in which this dialogue was made public.) Erasmus published it for the first time in the 1528 edition of his *Colloquies.* It was the year when he was most viciously assailed and tried by various inquisitorial courts. He stood alone, without sect or party to protect him; and he could not foresee that those condemnations would not be put into effect during his lifetime. But, instead of being intimidated, Erasmus renewed in this dialogue — with even more scorn and vigor — his indictment of the clergy, high and low. Their "unreligious religion" — of which he had accused them before and which he had attributed to their ignorance, in a greater degree than to their corruption — became now a "counterfeit of religion," purposely falsified by them in order to encourage war more effectively.

In spite of his age and his wretchedness, Erasmus' claws were still at their sharpest. But the author of *Charon* was no longer the Erasmus of *Peace Protests!,* the optimistic prosecutor who, simultaneously with his accusations and condemnations, hopefully showed rulers and clergy practical ways and means of installing permanent peace among nations. Now it was the disillusioned old man who, after all his endeavors to the contrary, saw mankind and Church plunged deeply into war of all kinds for many years to come, and who melancholically admitted his defeat.

In this dialogue, Charon confides to Alastor that he is somewhat worried about the writings of Erasmus on peace. Should that author, whom he calls contemptuously "a certain polygraph," succeed in his tireless propaganda, the flow of the dead towards the realm of the Styx would considerably diminish and the "boom" in the underworld, due to war, would come to an end:

CHARON: I was told that there dwells on earth a certain polygraph who does not stop using his pen to make men hate war and love peace.

ALASTOR: Pooh! For a long while now he has been singing his tune to deaf ears! Some time ago, he wrote *Peace Protests!*, or the complaint of the persecuted peace. But now he has just finished *The Epitaph* for the defunct peace. Besides, why don't you rather think of those who are working for our cause with no less zeal than the Furies themselves?

CHARON: Who are they?

ALASTOR: A certain species of birds, dressed in black or white cloaks, or in ash-gray robes — indeed, their plumage offers the greatest variety. You will find them always perched in the courts of the princes, tirelessly whispering in their ears the love of war and exhorting to the same end the mighty ones as well as the common people. In their sermons, they use the teachings of the Gospels to proclaim that war is a just, holy, and pious matter. But what I admire most about it, is . . . that they use exactly the same language in each of the opposing camps. In France, those preachers affirm that God is on the side of the French, and that those cannot possibly be defeated whom God himself assists in their fighting. In England and in Spain, they preach that God himself and not the Emperor, commands the armies. [*The ironical allusion to Charles V and to his military alliance with England in his war against Francis I, whom he made prisoner three years before, did not fail to produce in Spain the effect desired by its author. Juan de Valdés replied immediately with a refutation, "Diálogo de Mercurio y Carón," which was printed and rushed to the book markets with the greatest speed. Without naming Erasmus, the Spanish nationalistic humanist defended the Emperor, rejecting the entire responsibility for the raging wars upon his adversaries. When Erasmus' friend, the Spanish pacifist Juan-Luis Vives, published his Spanish translation of eight "Colloquies," including "Charon," its sale was promptly forbidden for political reasons. But, curiously enough, not Erasmus' edition in original Latin!*] Thus fighting even with no more than ordinary human courage would make their victory certain. Besides, any man who happens to fall in battle, far from being destroyed, will fly, with all his arms and armor, directly to Heaven.

CHARON: So much credit is given to what they say?

ALASTOR: What, I pray, cannot be obtained with a counterfeit of religion? To this add youth, inexperience, thirst for glory, resentment, at times a natural inclination towards the alluring end. It is easy to lay hands on those young men, and it is not hard to overturn a cart already inclining by itself towards the direction of its fall. . . .

CHARON: But what inflames them so much to preach war? What profit do they draw from it?

ALASTOR: Well, because they make more money on the dead than on the living — there are wills, funeral masses for the deceased, indulgences, and so many other sources of income which are far from being negligible. And — last but not least — they have more taste for life in military camps than in their monastic cells. War is bombarding *bishops* out of such men, who in time of peace were not worth a brass farthing. . . .

The last reproach — that not moral and spiritual achievements, but their military exploits, were often responsible for the elevation of priests to the dignity of bishops and cardinals — is the same which Erasmus addressed in *Peace Protests!* (See Note 15, page 191.) But then he asked no more than that "Priests . . . should never take part in war, except to end it." Now he was not satisfied with the rather passive role that he had hitherto assigned them. Henceforth, he demanded from them not only abstinence from war, not only the role of peace arbitrators, but the *immolation* of themselves.

It never ceased to surprise Erasmus that, while so many persons are ready to sacrifice their lives, whether from taste for adventure, or vice, or patriotism, from hatred or love, that there are none who would sacrifice themselves to preserve or re-establish peace when war has already begun. What struck him most was that such an individual was not to be found among the clergy, not even among those of them who sincerely devoted their lives to God. Could one better serve and spread the teachings of Jesus than by dying for peace? Why does no priest or bishop appear on the battlefield, between the two hostile camps, to attempt to stop the battle? Why, in a country at war, is such a peaceful crusade not undertaken by the churchmen, even at the risk of their lives? It was in this state of mind that, while Europe was bleeding from a thousand wounds, Erasmus, still pretending — in the interest of the cause — to regard Francis I (who did not stop inviting Erasmus to settle in France) as a friend of peace, while aware that he had become one of the greatest warmongers of the time, appealed to the King. The courage he revealed in this letter is admirable, for he addressed a mighty potentate on whom depended the carrying out of his condemnation by the Sorbonne, as well as the lives of his French friends who translated and circulated his works in France. And yet, through this letter to the King, Erasmus appealed to the clergy to oppose the sinister war activities of this same King and to induce his soldiers to disobey and to lay down their arms. For Erasmus soon made this letter public:

"If there has ever been," he wrote to Francis I among recommendations of how to stop war, including his cherished idea of international arbitration, "an opportunity for good shepherds to watch over the welfare of their flock at the risk of their lives; if there was ever an occasion to walk in the footsteps of that great Shepherd whose successors they claim to be, it is at the present hour when a deluge of crimes and calamities, fatal consequences of war, submerge our planet. Majesty, why, among so great a mob of priests, bishops, archbishops, and cardinals, is there not a single individual who dares to appear even at the risk of his life, to appease the bacchanal of war? What an honorable and happy death he would die who paid with his life for the sublime effort to save so many thousands of human lives doomed to frightful death by war!"

This letter is probably the most beautiful and — since it was made public by the author himself — the most courageous on which pacifist literature can pride itself. It continues to be translated into all civilized tongues and to be circulated either alone or with other writings of Erasmus against war. Although his recommendation that priests invade the battlefields, place themselves between the armies, and urge them to disobey and lay down their arms, was taken up afterwards, at various times, history does not tell us that the churchmen ever put into practice the exhortations of Erasmus. However, to Pope Benedict XV, a truly great and courageous pacifist, is attributed the intention of going onto the battlefields during the First World War, to stand between the enemy armies in order to stop the carnage.

As to the political ideas of Erasmus in general, they had a long-range effect. Taken up again in the seventeenth century by such men as Fénelon and Locke, they so conquered the best minds of England and France in the eighteenth that it would be difficult to imagine a Voltaire if Erasmus had never been. And I wonder whether the authors of the Declaration of Independence and the *Rights of Man* were not touched by the grace of Erasmus, and whether his spirit was not present at the proclamation of the United States of America, cradle, as its founders logically could have hoped, of the United States of the World. One finds traces of Erasmus in many of the great authors who devoted themselves to problems of government, democracy, war, and peace, and one sees his shadow on all the avenues of the social, political, and religious doctrines of democratic, equalitarian, cosmopolitan, and universalist tendencies.

Scholar though he was, Erasmus was neither sociologist nor economist nor philosopher in the modern sense. But he made precious contributions to all these sciences. With the prodigality of genius, too rich to analyze them one by one and force them into the framework of a system, he tossed his ideas to the winds without bothering to give them solid scientific or philosophic form that would crystallize their origin forever. Whatever his prodigious labors, he could not have accomplished more, even if he had wished to do so. Writers and thinkers of future generations have seized them and integrated them into their doctrines. Through these channels, long after people ceased to read the works of Erasmus in the original because of the inaccessible language in which they were written, many of his ideas have become part of the treasury of popular wisdom. It is because of their universal dissemination that, while often inspired by them, no one thinks of their source. This phenomenon is not true of Erasmus alone. It is to be observed in the daily wisdom of all peoples and all classes, in the proverbs we use, in the expressions with which we adorn our daily speech; their very popularity condemns them to anonymity. And so it is with some of the ideas with which Erasmus sowed the path of the future. Generation after generation, in the fight for peace, tolerance, justice, and brotherhood of peoples, we discover them on our forward march. And just as the brilliance of the light thrown on our forward path guides us but prevents us from seeing its source, so we are not aware to what extent we are indebted to Erasmus in our fight for a better world.

However, in the course of the centuries, a name has emerged by which we designate those who feel and think as

universalists, those who, though belonging to no party, look
to all of them for whatever they have that is good and constructive, just as the author of *Peace Protests!* considered himself a composite and refused to be only a part. That name
is *Erasmian,* and it constitutes the finest homage that our
little monk could have desired. Every fight against sectarianism, against fanaticism, against superstition and tyranny, in
political and spiritual, in religious and intellectual domains,
in whatever aspects they appear; every striving to unite in one
harmonious whole all that the spiritual and material world
has to offer — civilizations, religions, cultures, races — every
such fight is in its essence *Erasmian* and those who take part
in it are *Erasmians.*

"*The Sum of Religion*| *Is Peace*"

ERASMUS VERSUS LUTHER

AN ANALYSIS OF THE IDEAS of Erasmus on peace and of his fight for it would be only fragmentary if one were to omit the controversy between him and Luther. For centuries this has been the object of innumerable studies and divergent opinions, without its true meaning having emerged — the meaning, that is, which it could or even should have for our own times. For this controversy, if one regards it from the point of view from which the foregoing study of Erasmus' personality has been made, was caused not by differences of opinion on the urgent necessity of a reform — Erasmus himself furnished the elements and prepared the ground before Luther, his junior by seventeen years, even thought of them — but by their attitudes towards God and man, good and evil, humanism and violence, tolerance and persecution, peace and war. This is a major point and its importance at the present hour is more than historical.

To Erasmus, the fight for peace was closely allied with that for tolerance and freedom, without which peace would be only a mirage. But intolerance in the life of men is often a consequence of the intolerance to which the religious life has accustomed them. Seeking for an explanation of why a religion based on love for our neighbor and on peace can, from our earliest age, inculcate in us feelings so opposed to its principles, Erasmus discovered the source in its arbitrary dogmas.

94

For it was they which drove men to intolerance. He drew the conclusion that real religion should be *undogmatic* as far as possible; that is, as it originally was — in his opinion — before custom, superstitions, and theologians had corrupted it. Thence arose his scorn for theology, which he taxed with being a pseudo-science and the source of irreligion or rather, to quote him, of "irreligious religion and unlearned learning." Humanism offered the most potent means for changing it. It followed that whoever opposed humanism, or, by sowing trouble, made its diffusion impossible, was an enemy of peace.

To go farther: a dogmatic religion was necessarily intolerant and aggressive in the spiritual field, nor could it be pacific outside the Church. Indeed, can one be a pacifist in one thing and war-minded in another? Can one be a pacifist politically or militarily or socially, without first being so spiritually in relation to the single individual's religious conscience? No! For what is a pacifist? Erasmus, as we have seen, considered himself as a composite. And such was his conception of peace, which could only be a composite product and not an autonomous element. And as peace must be, so must be the man practising it. He accused political and religious parties of being but narrow parts. ("I love liberty, I do not wish and could never serve a party," he invariably replied from the beginning to the Lutherans who asked him to join them.) A true pacifist must be tolerant, must be liberal, and harmonize in himself the positive and constructive tendencies of all parties, all civilizations, and the truths of all creeds, the truth in its entirety not being a monopoly of any doctrine or church.

One is not a pacifist merely because he is against war — especially as long as the war has not started — nor is one a pacifist merely because he thinks he is. To become so truly, one must work at it, one must train a long time, one must go assiduously to the school of peace where one is both student and teacher. In short, one must learn the art of peace from everything in his daily life — just as, in order to tell the truth under all circumstances, it is not enough to believe oneself capable of it, but one must practise it constantly. Peace is every man's business and thus everything in life should become a training ground for tolerance and peace — our family, our social relations, religion, politics, arts, literature, lest we succumb to the nefarious intolerance which leads to violence and war. It has been said that we are the products of the books we read, but we are even more the products of the people who surround us, of the conversations which we hear from childhood at the table, and, to a large degree, of what is inculcated in us with the first religious principles. But religion has become a source of discord and violence. It therefore needs urgently to be reformed in order to become the great educator for peace. For — "what is religion if not peace?"

A reform whose goal was peace and understanding could only be pacific. Otherwise, it would be vitiated at its very foundation. It follows that, to be effective and widespread, a reform could not be undertaken by anyone who so desired, with any chance of its being generally accepted. It should come from above, that is, from the pope himself, whom everyone heeds. In the first years of Leo X's pontificate, Erasmus believed he had found this pope in him. He was convinced that he knew Leo's real thoughts, but that the Pope was unfortunately surrounded and ill-advised, like all autocrats. Consequently, he believed — and so informed Luther when the latter asked his advice — that, to change the existing order, he must attack only the cardinals, the clergy, the theologians, the monastic orders, their morals, the state of the Church and religion, its traffic in indulgences, and so forth, without involving the Pope. It would be the same thing, he added, if one wanted to reform the political regime in a country. The fight against the latter would be more effective if, placing the king above the disputes, one were to direct the whole attack against his government, his flatterers, and his advisers. By adopting the same strategy for a religious reformation, the moral authority of the Pope would not be lessened. When he was converted to the new ideas — and he must be — and ready to re-establish order, he alone could proclaim the new doctrine. He would then be the better heeded and everyone would be the more impressed because his name had not been sullied during the struggle.

As a friend of order, Erasmus saw in this strategy the only sure means of preventing violent upsets and of accomplishing a spiritual revolution. But, in case this revolution could not take place without provoking serious disorder and bloodshed, he would prefer to slow up until evolution itself would inevitably bring about the change because of the continual ideological struggle for it and the peaceful diffusion of new ideas. In other words, he was profoundly convinced that the prolonged contrast between the general state of enlightened minds and a superannuated regime would be as untenable as though — the comparison is that of William Ellery Channing — one were to insist on forcing adults to wear children's clothing; without the slightest violence, these clothes would burst at the seams.

Luther did not agree with Erasmus. Even if he had done so, his temperament would not have allowed him to conform. Ardent and fanatical soul, he was consumed by the fire of faith and by what he believed to be his duty toward God, both inciting to fanaticism and to martyrdom; whereas Erasmus had a horror of fanaticism under any guise and distrusted joyful martyrs, although admiring some of them. Doubtless he was aware that the person who, driven on by his fanaticism, was ready and even sought to endure torture under the conviction that God demanded it would be unlikely to attach value to the life of others when he attached so little to his own. That explains why the Inquisition could have been the work not of evil men but of profoundly pious men who were prepared to sacrifice themselves as burnt offerings. Indeed, the worst persecutors in the name of a God of love came from their ranks and, convinced that they were accomplishing an eminently religious action, they rejoiced in the spectacles where, for the so-called salvation of their souls, thousands of people were burned alive at the stake; they even envied the fate of their victims. To Erasmus, such fanaticism was a sacrilegious negation of the essence and purpose of religion. To make love triumph through intolerance and cruelty was a profanation which could only lead humanity to savagery and the abyss.

Although he had revolted against the tyranny of Rome, Luther, seeing God himself as violent, was a partisan of violence. And while he thundered against the tyrannical practices and certain dogmas of the Roman Church, and demanded from the pulpit and in his writings the largest possible tolerance and individual freedom in matters of faith, Luther, as soon as his uprising had succeeded and the existence of his new Church had been secured, proclaimed dogmas, introduced new rituals, imposed them by force, and persecuted dissenters. For the unmitigated triumph of his beliefs, he was ready to sacrifice the acquisitions of humanism, and he scoffed at those who trembled for the fate of culture and civilization. Although he passionately preached peace and denounced war as one of the greatest crimes against humanity, pacifism, as soon as his victory over Rome was certain, became the least of Luther's worries. He did not fear inundating his country with torrents of blood for the imposition of his will, and he did not hesitate to put to death those who opposed him. He even boasted of it. (See Note 10, page 189.)

Within a few years, the liberal author of *On the Freedom of a Christian Man* became the ruthless persecutor of all those who claimed for themselves that very same freedom which Luther so eloquently demanded. It was, however, that promise of religious freedom which, from the start of Luther's rebellion, was in great part responsible for his success, millions of men having joined him in his fight on behalf of freedom and against Rome which denied it. *On the Freedom of a Christian Man* was written and published at the end of 1520. Scarcely three years later, on August 2, 1523, Luther was still preaching from the pulpit the same freedom, denying to the national civil authorities the right to interfere with matters other than those exclusively worldly, as he denied to the Pope the right to interfere with religious individualism. But then, as soon as he had left the pulpit, he almost simultaneously urged the Elector of Saxony, who had saved his life and protected him against the Pope and the Emperor, to punish, to persecute, and to drive out of the country those who did not agree in all points with Luther's new creed and rituals. Thus, learning that the canons of the Collegiate Church in Wittenberg continued to celebrate the mass in spite of Luther's orders to the contrary, he asked the Elector to intervene against them and other heretics to his creed with all the power of the state, to forbid the mass by law and to punish dissenters.

Not a few of his originally most ardent disciples — as, for instance, Carlstadt, who himself demanded the abolition of the mass and who, in matters of creed, was far more radical than Luther in his best days — were shocked by this violent intolerance. In disgust, they turned their backs on the German Reformer, some of them even preferring to go voluntarily into exile rather than to bow to the Protestant Pope, as Luther was called, or to incur his wrath. But even the civil authorities were surprised not a little when Luther, after having denied to them for years the right to interfere with religious matters, suddenly enjoined them to become the watchdogs of the new creed. In their answer which has come down to us (see, in particular, the Weimar edition of Luther's *Werke*, XII, 649, and his letters edited by C. A. Burkhardt — *M. Luthers Briefwechsel, mit vielen unbekannten Briefen, etc.*, Leipzig, 1866, p. 76), they drew Luther's attention to his earlier recommendations and advised him not to contradict himself but rather to endeavor to serve as an example to his followers, remaining true to his own teachings and practising what he had long preached to others.

But Luther was not the man to be impressed by such reminders or to be troubled by the fact that his scandalous contradictions were apparent to every unprejudiced man. With his usual intransigentism, Luther insisted — and the Elector of Saxony, to whom he became the indispensable and most effective weapon against the heavy taxes and other exactions of the Pope, bowed to the Reformer's will; in return, the latter helped the civil authorities to break down ruthlessly the revolutionary uprising of the peasants. And yet the Peasants' War, as Erasmus did not fail to notice, would probably not have taken place without the encouragement found in the earlier teachings of Luther, himself a peasant's son.

Whatever the impression to the contrary, Luther, shrewd as he was, was not a hypocrite. In spite of his deliberate and open contradictions, and notwithstanding his undisguised *volte-face*, he was logical with himself. In his belief that there was no other will but that of the Heavenly Father, Luther resolutely followed his contradictory impulses and ideas with as much ruthlessness as apostolic candor. Criticisms and defections of some of his most prominent adherents left him unshaken in his belief that whatever he spoke, wrote or did, he was merely executing the commands of God. In his furious and coarse rebuke to Henry VIII, who had attacked his religious teachings, Luther called himself bluntly "the messenger of God" (in *Contra Henricum Regem Angliae*). To oppose Luther was to oppose God. God spoke through his mouth, God acted through him — he was but God's tool. His

role, as he explained it, was not different from a saw felling
a tree. The saw seems to be essential but, in reality, it is the
man who holds it who makes it accomplish his will and his
purpose.

Thus Luther was profoundly sincere when he considered
that everyone who disagreed with him was disobeying God
and therefore deserving of the adequate punishment which
the inspired Reformer was eager to inflict. Luther defended his doctrine and attitude with much eloquence and
persuasive arguments. But with all his genius he was unable
to grasp the most logical conclusion which his teachings suggested — that, if there be no personal will, those who opposed
Luther must have acted thus, too, by the will of God.

Later on Erasmus did not fail to emphasize this gap in
the logic of Luther, with much sarcasm and no less indignation. But knowing at first only Luther's spiritual motives, his
sincerity, his readiness to suffer for his convictions, Erasmus
could not foresee the rapid evolution of his ideas and beliefs,
still less his methods in imposing them, and not at all what
soon became his final goal. There is no doubt that Luther,
in the beginning, did not realize it himself. It was therefore
inevitable that the two champions of the Reformation should
soon appear in opposite camps.

The most casual parallel between these two great characters makes clear their complete incompatibility. They
were at the antipodes in nature as well as in mind. Luther,
subject to violent emotions, was guided by signs he thought
he saw and voices he believed he heard. He was ill tempered
and, by his own confession, never wrote or spoke as well
as when he was at the peak of rage: "In my prayers, in my
sermons, in my writings, I never succeed so well as when I
am very angry. For anger cools my blood, sharpens my mind,
and drives out assailing criticism." Erasmus, however, could
think and write only by concentrating so completely that he
forgot even the sharpest physical pain. He relied on reason

and, distrusting his emotions, he acted only after ripe reflection. Luther believed in the Devil, saw him with his own eyes, fought with him physically to such a point that one day, while working on his Bible translation into German, he seized the inkhorn from the desk and hurled it at the head of the Devil. (Still today, the guide in the Wartburg points out the ink spots to visitors.) But Erasmus mocked at the Devil and laughed at those who believed in him.

Luther became a monk not as a result of long meditations, but impulsively, because, while walking along the road of Erfurt, he saw lightning strike near-by without touching him. He regarded this as a sign from on high which he obeyed by taking orders. Erasmus, on the other hand, became a monk because he was forced to do so, and he was never reconciled to it. And he did not believe in signs nor in voices other than that of his conscience. Thus, walking one day in his garden in Basle, he heard a deafening explosion. Soon he learned that, struck by lightning, an arsenal had exploded and destroyed a part of the city, killing and injuring dozens of people. Its inhabitants saw in the calamity a divine punishment for their sins, or a foreboding of worse things to come. But Erasmus wrote to a friend: "I am more of a critic than a prophet." As such he could not see in the disaster any other meaning than that Christians, preparing war against other Christians, were stocking murderous ammunition, and that the careless city administration had been stupid and irresponsible enough to place a powder arsenal in the midst of a populated area.

Luther went on a pilgrimage to Rome. When he saw at a distance the Eternal City, he prostrated himself and kissed the soil. Erasmus went on horseback and as a tourist; from a distance he eagerly admired the panorama with its hills and monuments. The peasant Luther, visiting the Vatican and contemplating the palaces of the cardinals, was upset by the luxury in which the princes of the Church spent their easy lives. This spectacle seemed to him the incarnation of mortal sin and, naturally, contrary to the religion which they preached. Erasmus, while believing equally that the luxurious lives of the representatives of Jesus were not in conformity with Christian humility, smiled ironically. In any case, this luxury was not unknown to him. Long before going to Rome, he had on many occasions not only visited but lived in episcopal, princely, and even royal palaces. Besides, monk though he was, he was also an artist, and his indignation was softened by his boundless admiration for the exquisite taste, the love of art and the culture of these Roman cardinals, and he was enraptured with their collections and their libraries.

Erasmus knew human weaknesses and saw in the fleshly needs of man and his other desires something inherent in his nature, while Luther believed in temptations and was obsessed by them. Erasmus had an unlimited faith in man's creative energy and believed in progress. Luther believed in predestination and considered any human endeavor useless if God had not decided on it in advance. The optimism of the one and the pessimism of the other appeared even in their devotions: Erasmus, in praying, was sure that God, father of men, was always ready to hear him. Luther was not at all sure of it and, in praying, he often mourned and cried at the thought of appealing to deaf ears.

The two men were as unlike physically as morally. Erasmus was a tiny man with an ascetic's thinness — he ate almost nothing. Luther was corpulent, with a giant's build, and consumed enormous quantities of nourishment. Erasmus drank only fine burgundy; Luther, like a good German, drank beer. Being all of a piece, Luther knew only black and white, he loved tenderly or he hated ferociously, he was never indifferent. Whereas Erasmus was supple and, in his relations with people, his range of nuances was infinite. The language of Luther was remarkably powerful in its expression; when he attacked, his style became thundering and as deafening as a volcano, while Erasmus was gentle in manner, and in his attacks his weapon was a delicate irony that was the more to be feared when it was smiling. Erasmus was the product of the highest culture; Luther of the soil, an authentic part of nature. To Erasmus, faithfulness to the highest moral principles and a stainless life were the undeniable sign of the holiness of a man. He spoke of Saint Socrates and Saint Plato as naturally as he called the author of the Vulgate Saint Jerome. But Luther, learning that Zwingli, for whom he felt a profound affection, had expressed before his death (in his *Confession*) the hope of meeting in the Hereafter, reunited around Jesus, all the just and good men who had lived on earth — Socrates and other pagans among them — was filled with sorrow that his friend, as a result of such heresies, had probably destroyed any chance of going to Heaven.

Luther was an unbridled Jew-baiter. True, at the beginning of the Reformation, in the hope that they would embrace his new religion, he showed great friendship for the Jews, going so far as to flatter them. But later, seeing that his efforts were in vain, he turned violently against them and aroused the German people against the Jews to such a point that they had to appeal urgently to the civil authorities to protect them from Luther's provocations to violence. Erasmus, defending Reuchlin, the great Hebraicist of the Renaissance, remarked ironically that if persecuting the Jews and putting them to death were a sign of faithfulness to the teachings of Jesus, he had to admit that "we are all good Christians."

How could these two men — one subtle, the other gross; one smiling, the other gloomy; one celebrating man as the master of his destiny and of the future of humanity, the other proclaiming him a powerless tool — how could they have understood one another and followed the same road side by side to the end? And yet, both believed that they could do so. But from the first steps, Erasmus perceived that, in his opinion, Luther was on the wrong road, and he stopped short. The incompatibility of their natures, of their points of view, and of their goals, was so radical that even their cause could not be the same. And it was not.

Erasmus, with his unshakable faith in progress through peaceful evolution, was an evolutionist in matters of religion also. About God and religious truth he had an evolutionist theory of his own. In his opinion, no truth reveals itself at once, religious truth even less than any other. Genuine religion therefore escapes definitions which by their very nature can be applied only to what is static. Revelation in religion is constant, due to the growth of our knowledge about God and nature. Consequently, the logical conclusion of Erasmus' thinking could not be any other than that to him each new dogma was a violation of religious truth and a narrowing of God's greatness. "Thus God wished to make himself known to the human race by degrees only." That is indeed the conclusion of Erasmus himself in his diatribe against the Spanish inquisitors (in *Adversus Monachos quosdam Hispanos*) , who, accusing him of arianism and anti-trinitarianism, sought to condemn his works.

This is not the place to examine in detail Erasmus' views on religion. But he defined luminously what its spirit should be in a letter addressed on January 5, 1523, when the Lutheran revolt against Rome reached its peak, to John Carondelet, Archbishop of Palermo and Chancellor of Brabant: "The sum of religion is peace and unanimity [that is, universality]. And that is conceivable only if the definitions [that is, the dogmas] are as few as possible, and opinion left free to every one on many subjects. (*Summa nostrae religionis pax est et unanimitas. Ea vix constare poterit, nisi de quam potest paucissimis definiamus, et in multis liberum relinquamus suum cuique judicium.*) "

It seems to me that these few lines explain the conflict between Erasmus and Luther better than all the theological subtleties that the theologians and historians have gathered and examined so minutely over the centuries. If Erasmus could not concede that man might be a *part,* while his very nature commands him to be a *whole,* still less could he tolerate that the Church or religion should be anything but the largest synthesis, truly universal, excluding no authentic spiritual current.

Nevertheless, so long as the dispute between Rome and Luther was only doctrinal, Erasmus still continued to hope that this extraordinary man, with his genius, his energy, his courage, and his pure life, would be able to rise above himself, make his views universal, and achieve a Reformation from which humanity would benefit. *These two men never met.* But from the time Erasmus received Luther's first letter, overflowing with admiration — and even earlier — he poured out encouragement. Knowing the integrity of his motives, he took up Luther's defense against the calumnies and insults by which he was being answered. Erasmus used his finest ink in ridiculing the theologians who found nothing but insults with which to oppose the German Reformer. ("It is easy to call Luther filth but it is very hard to answer him.") And in almost all his letters, especially in those to influential prelates, popes, and kings, he praised Luther's life, his learning, the purity of his motives, and protested indignantly against his excommunication. Faithful to his tactics, Erasmus accused not the Pope but his entourage, whom he made responsible for the Pope's bull; and he warned the Supreme Pontiff himself against the serious consequences which would follow if the Holy See did not hasten to renounce violence and make peace with Luther. Since the Vatican's handling of Luther's case had hitherto had no other effect than to make things worse, the Pope dispatched to Germany Cardinal Campegio, his ablest diplomat, in the hope that the latter would succeed where his predecessors had failed.

The new apostolic envoy was a man of soft manners that appealed to Erasmus. Therefore, when the cardinal wrote to him asking for assistance and advice, Erasmus hastened to answer with a long letter, filled with the most salutary wisdom. But he seized also the opportunity to praise again Luther's life and motives, emphasizing at the same time his own devotion to the Roman Church, whatever its shortcomings. Thus the more vigorously could he denounce the corrupt life of the Catholic clergy and their slanders against Luther, the more persuasively could he insist on the urgency of an understanding with the German Reformer. "The Pope," Erasmus wrote to the cardinal, "has no worse enemies than his foolish defenders. He can reduce anyone to dust if he desires, but empires built on terror do not last. If we want truth, every man should be free to say what he thinks without fear. If the advocates of one side are to be recompensed with miters and those of the other with rope and stake, truth will not be heard."

Erasmus preached moderation to the Lutherans as to the Catholics. What mattered to him was to reform the Church as thoroughly as possible but without destroying its unity, the token of its future universality. He therefore called again and again upon both sides to elevate their debates, not to leave the field of ideas, to stop abusing one another. Otherwise, conceit and bitterness would be mixed up in them, violence would take the place of reason, and all serene discussion and agreement would become impossible. The result would then be not a Reformation but two hostile churches. He particularly deplored the violent character and grossness of Luther and in each of his replies, he warned Luther against himself. But all these endeavors and warnings served no purpose — as well try to grasp the whirlwind! The Lutheran

movement expanded and, with it, a lack of control on both
sides. Finally, they passed from insults to blows, and violence
was unleashed in both camps until Erasmus, disgusted and
losing hope, turned away from both of them.

Erasmus, the optimist, became morose. The apostle of
peace and of an undogmatic, universal religion saw with horror that in Germany there was developing a religious separatism which would open the dikes to an infinity of rival
creeds and sects. From these new churches he saw that there
would rise the most extravagant fanaticism, ready to set the
world on fire for the slightest theological divergence. With
religious sectarianism reinforcing national prejudices, he
saw the world drifting for centuries to come. To the customary imperialistic wars would be added religious wars; to
foreign wars, civil wars; to the Inquisition of Rome, "evangelical" inquisitions; each sect being convinced of alone knowing
the truth and alone being invested by God with the right
to massacre all those who thought differently. Human life,
so precious to Erasmus, was to become even cheaper than
it had been up to then.

What then was Luther's achievement as Erasmus saw it?
On the one hand, instead of accomplishing a reformation
within and freeing the Church of Rome of its chains, Luther
destroyed its unity but left it spiritually and intellectually in
the same state as before he revolted against it. On the other
hand, he raised a new church, equally dogmatic, equally
intolerant, equally contrary to humanism and peace, equally
tyrannical. And besides, while bringing no spiritual change
into the Catholic religion, he provoked in the ranks of its
adherents, as a comprehensible defense measure, a reactionary
movement, which would soon be known as the Counter-Reformation. Lutheranism was, therefore, for a free spirit, as
impossible to breathe as the dogmatism and theology of
Rome; while, at the same time, it forced the latter to become
increasingly rigid and stifling.

Lutheran separatism, retarding the realization of the Universal Church, meant, to the eyes of the humanist, a retrogression. But this was true not in the domain of religion alone. Luther's reform divided humanity, then and for a long time to come, more profoundly than had been the case before him. To Erasmus, therefore, Luther's success was not victory but defeat. And as his partisans celebrated their new religion as "evangelical" — in German, the official name of the Lutheran church even today is *Evangelische Kirche* — while the persecutions and pillaging perpetrated in his name raged in Germany, the far-sighted Erasmus wrote mournfully to a friend across the Rhine: "Formerly the Evangelist made savages gentle, criminals charitable, the avaricious pacific, those who cursed blessers. But these [the Lutherans], as though possessed, start revolts everywhere and incite good people to do evil. *I see new hypocrites, new tyrants arise,* but I do not see a single spark of the evangelical spirit." As for the popes and kings who, literally, implored him to take an active role on their side in the fight against Luther, he invariably replied: "I will never be a party to violence."

However, after having long refused, and only in the hope of being left in peace by Rome at least, Erasmus yielded to the demands of the Pope, as well as to those of Charles V, Francis I, and Henry VIII, who was still on good terms with the Holy See. Perhaps he would never have consented if Luther himself had not forced him to make this decision. Luther feared a strong attack from Erasmus, not only because he was the most powerful polemicist, as well as the most scholarly of his time, and because by taking his stand publicly and resolutely with that of Rome his name would bring considerable prestige to the latter, but also because Erasmus still had many admirers in the Lutheran ranks. But Luther knew, too, that if Erasmus disapproved of him, he approved no more of the conduct of Rome. Given the pressure which was constantly brought to bear on him from high places, it could be foreseen that, in spite of the great independence he enjoyed, Erasmus could not hold out in the long run. But Erasmus did hold out and he might have done so to the end, had not Luther made a bad error of judgment. The German Reformer notified Erasmus by letter that he would abstain from writing against him if he, Erasmus, would agree to keep still also. This was blackmail. And it revealed little knowledge of the "Prince of the Humanists." Erasmus immediately composed a little work, *On Free Will*, thus starting openly his campaign against the violent German Anti-pope. To Melanchthon he wrote privately, explaining the reasons that had led him, however reluctantly, to enter the public arena. Among these reasons, he said, Luther's blackmailing letter was the decisive factor.

Nonetheless, this attack was neither what Rome had a right to expect nor was it the violent criticism which the man of Wittenberg had every reason to fear. It was rather a symbolic act and its subject was academic. But it bore the stamp of its author's humanism and his faith in man. Erasmus addressed no reproach to Luther for having broken with Rome nor for having proclaimed a new religion, which he did not even discuss. He brought out only a single point which was as much philosophical as theological. If he drew largely on quotations from the Scriptures it was partly because of Luther, who based his doctrine on it, and partly because that was the style of the period. It was concerned with the question of free will as opposed to the fatalistic doctrine of Luther on predestination.

The question of free will has not ceased to preoccupy men since they began to think. From farthest antiquity to our own day, this problem has been debated, without lay thinkers or theologians having come to an agreement. Neither believers nor unbelievers have succeeded in offering a satisfactory answer and perhaps they will never do so. Is man free in action and independent in will? This question is not concerned solely with predestination. Do our education, our habits, our environments, our inheritances, our atavisms, allow us a really independent, free will? We believe so when we think before making a decision and conform our actions to it. To this many philosophers and all the skeptics reply that there is no certainty that our decisions would not be different if our habits and our inheritances did not prevent us from thinking differently from the way we do. Whereas in religion predestination denies man all power of initiative: whatever he does is conditioned by the fate given man at his birth, and whatever he accomplishes on earth, whether good or evil, is independent of his will, unless grace touches him and changes the course of his destiny.

This doctrine, when carried to an extreme as in Islam, constitutes what is popularly called fatalism, and in philosophy, on a cosmic or scientific scale, determinism. Judaism, through the most authoritative post-Biblical mouth of Maimonides, rejects this doctrine as impious, because it degrades man to the level of an animal, makes his reason superfluous, and makes of the Supreme Being an immoral being — which is blasphemy. For it would take an immoral being to punish crimes and sins which man could not help committing, while rewarding meritorious actions which were not a result of virtue acquired at a cost of effort and heroic abnegation. In Christian theology, several parallel currents have been manifested since the first centuries of its existence, one of them admitting free will, another denying it, and a third taking the middle ground, declaring that the human will was free in some things and subject to God's Will in others. The three currents were defended with equal authority by the most eminent fathers of the Church. The darkest expression of the negation of free will which Protestant Christianity offers is not, however, that of Luther but that of Calvin, in spite of all the efforts of his disciples to soften it.

For his part, Erasmus analyzes this question in two aspects — theological and philosophical. Theologically, he considers the denial of free will as contrary to the teachings of the Scriptures about reward and punishment. The denial of free will is immoral because it calumniates God to whom, in that case, one could attribute all the evil and all the crimes perpetrated on earth, while he punishes the so-called sinners. "If man," Erasmus says, "has no right to be considered the author of his good works, one cannot regard him as the author of his evil ones." But if, contrary to our conception of the most elementary justice, he must be so considered, as Luther said, the worst of criminals would become an innocent victim, a martyr, because predestined to crime in spite of himself. In that case, the divine commandments would have no meaning and all the moral teachings of religion would be only revolting hypocrisy. To deny the logic of such a conclusion is to fall into paradox. But in that case, a single paradox would not suffice, because "to defend this paradox one would have to rely on many others," until one would make of the Heavenly Father "a God more cruel than the famous Dionysius, tyrant of Sicily."

It is the same thing when one regards this doctrine from the point of view of philosophy or applied morals. By attributing to predestination all man's conduct and all his actions, one would kill all spirit of initiative in him, all creative effort; one would destroy in man his faith in progress, one would make him despair of the future of humanity, since he could not even make a contribution to it. In short, any effort to abolish the scourges of humanity — famine, sickness, poverty, crime, war — would become useless, and the creative energies of man would slowly become atrophied. It is possible, on the other hand, that will is not free in all cases, and Erasmus implies that in his opinion the truth doubtless lies between the two extreme affirmations. But this middle ground does not encroach on human dignity. Finally, our spirit of charity would prevent us from spreading among the people so exclusive a doctrine as that of Luther. To deny free will categorically is to drive men into despair.

Erasmus, with his faith in reason and thus in a better future for humanity, with his conviction that God is all goodness, that religion is here to make us all good and just, thanks to the moral principles that it inculcates in us and makes us obey, that a better world depends in large measure on men themselves and that God is always present to aid them — Erasmus, with all these views, could not tolerate the defeatist teachings of Luther on the role of man.

To sum up, *On Free Will* was the work of a philanthropist rather than that of a critic, the enlightened discussion of a friend who raises his own arguments rather than the attack of an adversary who condemns without appeal. Far from its being the diatribe of a demagogue, Erasmus even admitted that he could be wrong and that in such a case he would be grateful to Luther to instruct him. If Luther's paradoxes, Erasmus added in his conclusion, "are well founded, I would be the first to recognize the tardiness of my own mind, because I do not understand them. . . . I do not hold here the role of judge. . . . Although weighted with years, I am not and I will not be ashamed to learn from a younger man if he teaches me more obvious things with evangelical charity."

Indeed, the tone of the author could not have been more conciliatory and he invited Luther to follow his example and answer him, in the interests of truth, with equal amiability. But Luther, mad with rage, replied in an enormous volume, *The Enslaved Will,* in which he showered Erasmus with insults, while admitting in the beginning (which probably only increased his rage) that Erasmus was the only one of his critics to discover the central — we would say, the weakest — point of his doctrine. It is true that, immediately after its publication, Luther hastened to send him a friendly letter in which he excused himself for having treated him somewhat rudely, explaining his rudeness by his stormy temperament. But Erasmus' disgust was complete. He did not want to maintain personal relations with a man incapable of controlling his passions, who even declared that he was not responsible for his anger. Erasmus replied with a letter breaking off their relations, moderate in tone but not softening his words. He wrote:

"I am not so naïve that a humbug can reconcile me to all the wounding things that you have written and that you hoped would destroy me, or that a caress can make me forget everything. You say that you are a man of violent temperament. But what have all your many ridiculous insults, all your unscrupulous lies — that I do not believe in God, that I am an Epicurean, a skeptic who questions the Christian faith, a blasphemer, and I don't know what else — what have all these to do with the subject?

"I prefer not to dwell on what you owe me nor on the return that you have made me. That concerns me alone. As for you, I would wish you another mind if you were not so well satisfied with the one you have. As for me, you are free to wish me anything you like with the exception of your mind, unless God should endow you in the meantime with a new one."

From this point on, there was open war between the two men. Erasmus withdrew "on the rock of Saint Peter until peace returns." It was the reign of violence and he realized his impotence. Already, in his work *On Free Will* he had warned Luther that he was not a gladiator made for the arena. And elsewhere he confessed that he was not made for martyrdom either. In withdrawing from the battlefield, he wrote to an old English friend, there was nothing dishonorable: "When we can do no good, we have the right to keep silent." But it was only a relative silence. Erasmus replied in several pamphlets in which he made Luther feel his claws more sharply than ever before. Then, while not taking part in the struggle, he expended himself up to his death in efforts, constantly calling on the two opposing parties to find some meeting ground — in the interests of the Church, of peace, of the future of humanity. But none wished to hear him. A flood of insults thundered endlessly against him, particularly from Luther after he knew that Erasmus was definitely lost to his cause. He called him a "pornographer," a "venemous polemicist," a "bug," a "pig of an Epicurean," a "gossip," a "sophist," an "ignorant man," and so forth. And as, along with these insults, there came to Erasmus from Germany still other depressing news, notably about the civil war which already had taken a toll of thousands of victims, he replied that he would prefer "rather to be a simple sheep lost in the flock of Saint Peter than to lead a band of pigs." To Melanchthon, the most faithful, influential, and cultivated disciple of Luther, who continued to venerate Erasmus and to correspond with him until his death, he wrote, alluding ironically to his master's belief in the Devil: "The Devil is a clever fellow. A success like that of Luther would turn the head of the most modest of men."

Wrapped in disdainful silence, Erasmus returned to his humanistic labors. But in spite of the right which he claimed to keep silent, he was soon driven into breaking it. He declared that henceforth his role would be only that of a neutral spectator. But could he do it? His so-called neutrality was not that of a man who had become indifferent or undecided between two parties, but that of a free man who had his own opinion and did not conceal it. Was he not the declared enemy of both rather than one of them, and thus exposed to the attacks and blows of both adversaries? To be with neither one, which meant being against both — these violent times would not allow or pardon such independence of mind. Our own times illustrate it every day with violence enough. Thus Erasmus was accused until his death — and even up to our own days — by some of being a "Papist," by others of being a Lutheran or of having "laid the egg" from which Luther emerged. (Or rather, "Erasmus laid the egg which Luther hatched," as quoted by Erasmus.)

Erasmus endured the fate of the independent man who hates violence. Meanwhile, the civil war raged in Germany. In Catholic countries, the Counter-Reformation and the Inquisition grew out of bounds. Across the Channel, Henry VIII broke with Rome. Doubtless encouraged by the success of Luther — against whom, however, he had been, not so long ago, the only crowned prince to write a book — the king of England, in his turn, founded a national religion and proclaimed himself its head. Intransigently intolerant toward everybody who refused to join his Church, he beheaded, among many other outstanding men, one of his greatest subjects and most devoted servants, Sir Thomas More, Erasmus' dearest friend. Shortly before More, another of his friends, Berquin, had been burned alive in Paris as a heretic, although the young Frenchman's greatest heresy had been translating into French some works of his master Erasmus, whom the Inquisition did not dare touch. Indeed, Rome even offered him the cardinal's hat which he hastened to decline. His inner solitude became immense. More of a pacifist than ever, he clung to the rock of Saint Peter, in the conviction that, in spite of all its defects and its shortcomings, the Church of Rome still offered better conditions for the Reformation on an universal scale than the new Church of Luther — a solid ground on which one day could be built the universal religion, a prelude to the free universal state, since by addressing all mankind it was, at that time, the only church that did not run the danger of becoming separatist or nationalistic.

Certain partisan interpreters and biographers of Erasmus, after calling him a liar, hypocrite, egotist, ingrate, psychopath, have been eager to see in his final decision a complete endorsement of the Roman creed. Others have gone so far as to claim that Erasmus recanted. Others again have gone even farther, affirming positively that Erasmus died as a pious, orthodox Catholic, provided at his demand with the last rites. How did they learn this? Because his youngest secretary was a priest, Erasmus, they say, asked him to administer the last sacraments! But there is nowhere — in the records left by his friends — the least hint to support such an assertion. For over three centuries nobody ventured to affirm it. Only as late as 1842 did a Belgian priest, Mgr. de Ram, publish a study in which he "proved," after a long research, that Erasmus' secretary, who was at his bedside when he died, had administered the last rites to him.

It must be said that scarce are those even among Erasmus' partisan biographers who, after 1842, made much use of that sensational "discovery." Whereas no one of his friends, who for days surrounded the slowly dying Erasmus and recorded all the details, even his last words (suddenly spoken in Dutch, his mother tongue, which they never heard him speak before), ever mentioned or even alluded to it. Not even Beatus Rhenanus — his spiritual executor and most admiring disciple, who came to Basle to live near his master and to whom we owe the first posthumous publication of Erasmus' complete works as well as the only two biographical sketches of their author, written by a contemporary — recorded a single word about the performance of the last rites. There is no trace of it in Rhenanus' first biographical sketch, written shortly after the death of Erasmus, in 1536, and addressed to the Archbishop of Cologne. Nor does he mention such an important fact in his second biographical sketch (written four years later and addressed to Charles V), with which he prefaced the posthumous edition of Erasmus' complete works

in 1540. There is not a word about it, although Beatus
Rhenanus must have known how pleased Charles V would
be to learn that his late counsellor, so often accused and
tried by his inquisitorial Holy Office as a heretic, had died
as a thoroughly orthodox son of the Roman Catholic Church.
Even if Beatus Rhenanus had, surprisingly enough, not
been present, as some of his partisan biographers assume,
at Erasmus' bedside, when he was provided with the last
sacraments, he would still have learned about it from the
priestly secretary himself or from other intimate friends,
who kept a constant watch by their dying master.

And why, long before his death, knowing that in Basle
Catholic burials were no longer made, had Erasmus himself
not asked to be buried elsewhere — for instance in Freiburg,
where he had just spent several years, where he wrote his
so-called recantation and which remained Catholic throughout — if that ritual would have been of such importance to
him? If such had been his supreme desire, Erasmus' friends,
Catholics and Protestants, no doubt would have respected
and complied with it as faithfully after his death as they
complied with his wishes during his lifetime. Thus Erasmus
was buried in the most distinguished place which his friends
and the city of Basle could have found for his last rest: the
Protestant cathedral. Even later on, for centuries, no claims
were ever made by Catholic admirers — and these were not
wanting! — that his remains should be transferred to a Catholic burial ground. If such a claim had been supported by a
really unquestionable proof, even now the city of Basle
would comply with Erasmus' last wish, the more so as that
Protestant city has again its Catholics and its Catholic
cemetery.

In my opinion, such assertions are no more than wishful
thinking. The truth is that nothing can do more injustice
to the real thought and the final position of Erasmus between
Rome and Luther than conclusions of this kind. The cling-

ing of Erasmus to the "rock of Saint Peter" was of a quite different character, and a genuine Erasmian one. In his public rebuttals of Luther's attacks (in *Hyperaspistes*), Erasmus, with a marvelous frankness and always endeavoring to put himself above personal resentment, declared that he would quit the Church of Rome as soon as a better religion was offered to him. (Literally: "Therefore, I endure this Church till the day I shall see a better one." *Fero igitur hanc Ecclesiam donec video meliorem.*) His decision was thus not irrevocable. Indeed, he did not cease to deplore that Luther had not succeeded in performing a real Reformation, that which Erasmus craved and struggled for, a world creed which would unite mankind instead of dividing it more than before, a free religion which would create unanimity among men, the only religion worthy of God. "If you were able to persuade me that you really are the God-sent man," he wrote in *Hyperaspistes,* "I would crawl on my hands and knees, *without hesitation,* as far as Wittenberg and kiss your feet."

Moreover, in spite of having broken with the German reformer and notwithstanding so many insults and bitter words, in spite also of his real aversion, Erasmus still kept in his heart a genuine sympathy with certain sides of Luther's rich personality, and even a strong feeling of solidarity with him, a solidarity which, whether the two men liked it or not, still bound them together in their struggle against Rome. Erasmus admired Luther's greatness, which was real, as well as his occasional goodness, which was genuine; but he was at the same time repulsed by his opponent's meanness, even viciousness and cruelty towards those who disagreed with him. "I admire in Luther," Erasmus confessed, "the co-existence of two persons radically opposed. At times, I feel in him the true apostolic inspiration; and on the other hand, in his jokes, in his sarcasms and insults, he outdoes the buffoons . . . as if forgetting the drama he is playing and the role he has in it." And whatever his grievances against the new Lutheran creed, he expressed repeatedly his fears for its founder's life and how disastrous it would be if Rome succeeded in crushing Luther: "The destruction of Luther would deprive us of a precious good."

Thus it is clear that, whatever his official church affiliation may have been, Erasmus kept his spiritual freedom until the very end. If such a complex spiritual attitude as his were susceptible of any framing formula, the latter would still be found not among official church denominations but in the utterances of its most faithful interpreter — in Erasmus himself. To him, peace among men, justice, goodness, purity of life, spiritual fervor, moral commandments — all the good things for which Erasmus struggled — cannot, by their very universality, be the prerogative of any exclusive creed. From that point of view, the new religion called Lutheran, with its tyrannical dogmatism, could satisfy him as little as, and even less than, the Roman creed, in which at least he was born and which claimed universality and tradition. Free men guide and are willing to be guided, wrote Erasmus. "Asses are driven. Tyrants drive."

Erasmus was a free man.

Such in brief are the various phases and causes of the controversy which engaged Erasmus and Luther for the greater misfortune of future generations. Erasmus, the greatest humanist of the Renaissance and its most lucid intelligence, the world citizen, the apostle of peace and tolerance in all domains, the friend of man and of progress — on the one hand. On the other, Luther, fanatically inspired by his new faith and implanting it with violence, authoritarian himself in matters of belief and also exacting from his fellow citizens complete submission to the ruling civil authority. Luther was the greatest religious agitator since Mohammed and doubtless the greatest German of all time. The greatest, because, for better or worse, none of their sons has left a stronger stamp on the character of the German people, and also because he gave Germany its literary masterpiece, the translation of the Bible. And with their Bible, Luther endowed all German-speaking peoples with the same literary, unifying language.

I have endeavored to sketch Luther's moral portrait as seen in the light of Erasmus. Nevertheless, before the reader forms a definite opinion of this extraordinary man, in connection with the part he played in the formation of the German character and in world history, one would do him perhaps the greatest justice by quoting the late Gerhart Hauptmann, the outstanding German dramatist of our century: "Luther's good qualities acted upon [the Germans] too little, his faults too much." (*Gesammelte Werke,* by Gerhart Hauptmann, Berlin, 1922, Vol. XII, p. 80.)

To sum up, as far as Erasmus is concerned: in all this controversy, he was guided by no other considerations than those resulting from his uncompromising universality and his all-out pacifism. He opposed Luther because of his conviction that violence engenders more violence and perpetuates it, as surely as each war engenders more wars, and pushes peace constantly further off; because of his belief in the most intimate interdependence between freedom and peace, neither of which is capable of existence without mutual support; because of his deepest conviction that universal religion, creating unanimity through free consent, is as natural for the individual as a federated world state, putting an end to wars, is natural for nations. And he opposed Luther because of his belief that dogmas and definitions in religious matters, besides perpetuating exclusiveness and thus provoking it on an always larger scale, do violence to the very nature of religion — God being the Father of all mankind, and religious truth being constantly submitted to the same principles of evolution as the growth of the most diversified human knowledge.

Luther's approach was a theological one. But, for Erasmus, theological subtleties counted for little, and the real stake of the debate surpassed in importance all that theology — which through centuries became its most authoritative judge and historian — believed or was capable of seeing in it.

For the author of *Peace Protests!*, what was involved was neither more nor less than the future of humanity. By trying to present it and explain it today as it has been traditionally done — as a purely theological divergence of views on certain particularities of faith — one would narrow this great debate and falsify its meaning, for one would strip it of its tragedy and its magnificence. Magnificent, because of its grandiose unfolding and its stake, it not only was tragic for Erasmus himself and for his times but became so, by its consequences, for centuries to come. For that was one of the rare hours in the existence of mankind when it would have been possible to realize its greatest dreams, dreams of universal peace in all fields. At that moment, all the spiritual and temporal powers were hanging on the lips of Erasmus and Luther, and one may speculate on what would have resulted from an understanding between these two extraordinary men, the genius of thought and the genius of action.

At the time, Luther won out over Erasmus, but Erasmus was far from being vanquished. The great debate of Erasmus against Luther did not begin with them, it was not interrupted after them, and it continues today under many names with all its vigor.

In truth, it is the debate of our times.

PART TWO

PEACE PROTESTS!
by Erasmus of Rotterdam

For their individual safety as well as for the common interest, the neighboring states should make a kind of general League or Republic. . . . If every citizen owes much to his country, how much more each nation owes for even stronger reasons to the safety and peace of the Universal Republic in which are gathered all the countries of individuals.

FRANÇOIS (DE SALIGNAC DE LA MOTHE) FÉNELON, Archbishop of Cambrai (France), (1651-1715), in *Duties of Royalty* (*Devoirs de la Royauté*)

If I had known anything that would be useful to my country but detrimental to Europe and detrimental to the human race, I would have looked upon it as a crime.

CHARLES DE MONTESQUIEU (1689-1755) in *The Spirit of the Laws* (*L'Esprit des Lois*)

The age needs nothing more than peacemakers, men of serene, commanding virtue, to preach in life and word the gospel of human brotherhood.

WILLIAM ELLERY CHANNING (1780-1842) in *The Present Age*

Translator's Introduction

"Each generation must translate for itself." — T. S. Eliot

Peace Protests! is, to my knowledge, the first *complete* translation of the *Querela Pacis* of Erasmus to be made in English since that of Thomas Paynell appeared, under the title of *The Complaint of Peace* in London in 1559; this was the first and has remained the only one. Those published since 1559 have been only reproductions when they were not plagiarisms. While certain persons claimed that they were offering a new translation of the work of Erasmus, they provided, at most, a good editing job and modernized transcriptions of the Paynell version. Their very errors betray their source. On the other hand, a number of extracts or abridgments of this work have been translated on various occasions and distributed as tracts, either as pamphlets or added to other texts on peace which were not always those of Erasmus.

The translation of Thomas Paynell is, for the most part, still remarkable for its exactness. That is not its least merit when one recalls that during the epoch in which his translation was made, people bothered little about exactness of terms or even of meaning. Particularly in cases where the author shaded his thought and, in order to forestall the vigilance of the authorities, expressed himself by allusions, the latter are often lost when the translator either failed to, or dared not, make them sufficiently transparent, as Erasmus had done. For in that age, it required uncommon courage to avow that one was the translator of a work like *Querela Pacis*. In France, for example, the translation appeared very soon but, aside from the name of Erasmus, it bore neither the name of the translator nor that of the printer, nor of the place nor even the year. And yet there is no doubt that it was the work of Berquin, the young French friend and avowed translator of various works of Erasmus, who was condemned to death and burned alive in Paris during the lifetime of his master. The fate of Berquin could not have encouraged his emulators, although there were men courageous enough to publish translations in Spanish and in German a few years after the printing of the original. It is significant that the first English translation of *Querela Pacis* was not published until forty-two years after its Latin version.

In spite of its qualities, however, this translation has certain shortcomings. The fine Latinist was guilty of some gross errors to the detriment of the text of Erasmus. An example: Paynell translated *at is cupiebat etiam,* etc. (which, speaking of the Emperor Octavius-Augustus, literally means, *but he was willing even* or *and yet he desired even*) by *Atis also desired,* supposing that "Atis" was a mythological or real hero of antiquity, without inquiring whether this name had ever figured anywhere else.

In addition, the Paynell translation was made either from the text brought out by Frobenius, in December, 1517, or from one of the pirated reprints, which often swarmed with errors. A modern translator may have recourse to the so-called definitive edition, *Desiderii Erasmi Roterodami Opera Omnia,* Lugduni Batavorum (Leyden), 1703-1706, Editio Clericus (LeClerc), 10 volumes. But today even that is far from final, thanks to important corrections which have been made in the texts of Erasmus during the last two centuries.

That "definitive" text of *Querela Pacis* differs little from the first edition and these small differences consist only in variations of style, shades of meaning sometimes too delicate to be perceived at a first reading. But they become important when one proposes to make an up-to-date translation. His students know how meticulous Erasmus was in his choice of words, and that he constantly revised his published works for new editions. A word — or even a tense — changed was often a new light, formerly shadowed for reasons of security. How can a translator ignore it?

The principal source of my translation is the Clericus or LeClerc edition. But I constantly compared the text with that of various editions which appeared during the lifetime of the author. Whenever one word or grammatical form seemed to me more Erasmian than another, I freely made the choice; and I took the same liberty in rendering the rhythm, the style, or the atmosphere of the work. For the task which I imposed upon myself consisted in transposing not only the text from one language into another, but also, as far as possible, the atmosphere of a distant century into that of our own. This method, of course, occasionally involved the omission of a word whose meaning has become strange for the modern reader, and even, in one case, the omission of several lines — those concerning the Turks and the projected crusade against them (page 171).

On the other hand, every translator from classical languages is confronted by a phenomenon of linguistic expansion. There are expressions in Latin which, translated into English, do not give all the richness if one insists on reproducing them in as brief and concise a form as that of the original. There are words which can be rendered only by several others, words which sometimes become phrases. Otherwise, the translator would be juggling with the meaning or making unrecognizable the style and originality of the author. That is because modern tongues are more loquacious than the classical languages. Is that a sign of richness, of greater precision? Perhaps, though it has yet to be proved. However, even if a translator were to succeed in making our modes of expression conform to the economic brevity and conciseness of the ancients, without altering the meaning, the language would become so artificial that it would be even heavier than bookish. This would do violence to natural speech as well as betray the author. For the style and rhythm of Erasmus are essentially narrative — the spoken word. A fascinating talker, he wrote in a style that was a natural continuation of his familiar conversation. The secret of his art as well as the literary modernism of Erasmus consist largely in the fact that he rejected a bookish language.

To translate word for word, for reasons of alleged exactitude, this flaming indictment by Peace, to frame it in the English of our day as Erasmus expressed himself in Latin in 1516, without taking into account the intentions of its author or that the work, addressed to the whole world, brings a burning actuality to bear on these problems, would really be to distort it. At the same time it would confirm the opinion of Erasmus on cerain translators, as well as the correctness of the old Italian dictum, which made them the equivalent of traitors: *Traduttore, traditore* (translators, traitors).

Finally, in providing it with annotations, and by delving deep in research, and having submitted myself to the scientific discipline the work demanded, I did not aspire to make this *primarily* a scholarly work. What was important to me was to make it accessible to any reader. That is — as I have already indicated at the beginning of my study on *Erasmus: Herald of a United World* — I have not translated *Querela Pacis* because it is a literary masterpiece or because it has historical interest, but with the profound conviction that Erasmus' manifesto still addresses and appeals powerfully to our generation and that, by making him speak the language of our time, it will fill a void.

Fill a void!

In saying that, I do not forget the many excellent works that have appeared on the problems which weigh so heavily on humanity today, particularly those in which the authors try to solve them, offering ingenious projects for averting the grave dangers with which our generation and the future of our civilization are menaced. And yet, in spite of their

good will, their sincerity, and their idealism, our political
writers, pacifists, critics, moralists, and thinkers have not
succeeded in producing a work that would serve as the adequate cry of our consciences. The void is there. It gapes
particularly wide when we take account of contemporary
creative literature — fiction, whether novel, drama, or cinema.
The problem of peace — that is, the problem which weighs
most heavily on the minds, consciences, and emotional life
of our generation — find scarcely an echo there, and this
phenomenon is not limited to the literature of our country
alone. The longings for a better tomorrow, our nostalgia
for peace, our hopes fixed on the United Nations — none of
these has inspired, since the end of the Second World War,
a single best seller in the domain of fiction. It is not that our
epoch lacks good writers. But it seems as if our great contemporary authors, or those who pass as such, no longer "de-
mean" themselves to put their talents at the service of
peace.

Whatever the reason, the fact remains that, among the
finest works of the last decade, fiction and non-fiction, there
is not one which can equal *Peace Protests!*, I do not even
say in genius, but in universality, in emotion, in frankness,
in the precision of its targets, in indignation, in moral greatness, and — last but not least — in *courage*. Read the page in
which Erasmus analyzes, phrase by phrase, the meaning of
the Lord's Prayer in the mouth of a soldier on the point of
engaging in deadly battle; listen to the indignant, accusing
voice whose pathos recalls, at times, that of the Greek tragedies. Then say what novel of our day, what drama, what
film, what musical composition can claim to have dealt in
the last years with so *universal* a subject in its frightful actuality, a subject that concerns equally the human race of all
continents, all peoples, all classes, as well as each individual
in himself?

Indeed, the pacifist manifesto of the heroic monk lends

itself admirably to filling the gaping void. Perhaps this work will inspire others who can satisfy our needs even better than Erasmus. Anyway, the first duty of the translator was to give the author's text an expression and an intonation as modern as his ideas. I only regret that I dared not replace the facts which are no longer of our time, or the personages who belong to the past, by facts and names more familiar to our ears. Let any reader make his own substitutions as suggested by the text. In reading *Peace Protests!*, this substitution operates of itself, just as its contents suggest many parallels between the age of Erasmus and our own, to make it the book of our time.

José Chapiro

Preface

GREETINGS, Philip, venerable Bishop, no less illustrious for
your noble virtues than for the majesty of your ancestors. I
would congratulate you on being raised to so high a dignity
were I not certain that you accepted it reluctantly and that,
in undertaking this noble employment, you were influenced
only by the authority of our illustrious Prince Charles, your
relative, so affectionately expressed that you could not resist
it. Your lack of haste in accepting this post confirms my
certainly that you will acquit yourself with honor, con-
sidering that Plato, the great sage whose judgment was truly
divine, believed that the men most capable of governing a
state are those who agree only reluctantly to assume the
responsibility.

However, my confidence in your wisdom increases every
time that I recall the worthy brother whom you are succeeding and the noble father whose sons you both are. For
your brother David, with his great erudition and wisdom,
raised by his good deeds both episcopal dignity and his own
name to the peak of glory, when he governed this same
bishopric for several years. Great and worthy in all his
actions, he was still more so by his love for the public welfare, and he stated that nothing is more important to the
state than peace. In that he imitated your noble father
Philip, Duke of Burgundy, that great prince, rich in all the

---

1 References are to the Translator's Notes beginning on page 185.

virtues, who made his name immortal, especially because of having cultivated the *art of peace*.

May you follow this fine example and imitate these noble virtues, not only as a son but as a prince.

Your wisdom leads you to understand what the whole world expects of you. You bear on your shoulders a triple burden: the examples of your father and of your brother, and the fatality of these gloomy times which are leading, I hardly know why, toward war. Have we not seen just recently how certain persons, true enemies of peace and more hostile to their friends than to their enemies, have overlooked and avoided nothing to bring about the war? On the other hand, we have seen those who, devoting themselves with all their hearts to the welfare of the state and their prince, have succeeded, at a cost of so many difficulties, in making us understand that peace with France, always desirable, was more than necessary now.

Indignant at these facts, I decided to write *Peace Protests!*, seeking in this way to appease the natural grief of my soul or to avenge it.

I am, therefore, sending you this book as a tribute due to the new Bishop, so that Your Excellency may cultivate peace at whatever cost, for I could not adjust myself to the idea that one can forget all the troubles that war has cost us.

Farewell!

DES. ERASMUS OF ROTTERDAM

Peace Protests!

I

If, in spite of my innocence and regardless of the advantages which I offer them, men hate me, drive me away, and discredit me, nothing remains for me but to deplore the affront they offer me and their iniquity. But in repulsing me as they do — I who am the source of all happiness on earth — they attract and bring upon themselves the worst misfortunes. Thus should I not rather pity their fate than deplore the outrage they do me? However natural may be my inclination to bear them ill will, I am nonetheless forced to have compassion on them and to pity their horrible fate. Indeed, cruel as it may be to repulse him who, in whatever manner, reveals his devotion for another, it is still more ungrateful to disdain him who deserves to be showered with rewards. But, after all, this persistence in desiring their lamentable fate and in not recognizing the superiority of the advantages that I bring with me, this obstinacy in bringing down upon themselves the worst calamities that rend the world — is it not rather the peak of madness?

Yet, while it is natural and just to despise and punish criminals, we can only pity those who are possessed by madness. And they are the more to be pitied because they do not even perceive that they themselves are the instruments of their own ills and that nothing in the world can make them realize the enormity of their folly.

If I am truly that peace so extolled by God and by men;
if I am really the source, the nourishing mother, the pre-
server and the protector of all the good things in which
heaven and earth abound; if, without me, no prosperity can
endure here below; if nothing pure or holy, nothing that is
agreeable to God or to men can be established on earth without my help; if, on the other hand, war is incontestably the
essential cause of all the disasters which fall upon the universe and this plague withers at a glance everything that
grows; if, because of war, all that grew and ripened in the
course of the ages suddenly collapses and is turned into ruins;
if war tears down everything that is maintained at the cost
of the most painful efforts; if it destroys things that were
most firmly established; if it poisons everything that is holy
and everything that is sweet; if, in short, war is abominable
to the point of annihilating all virtue, all godliness in the
hearts of men and if nothing is more deadly for them, nothing more hateful to God than war — then, in the name of
this immortal God, I ask: Who is capable of believing without great difficulty that those who instigate it are still men?
Those who barely possess the light of reason, those whom
one sees exerting themselves with such stubbornness, such
fervor, so much cunning and at the cost of so much effort and
danger, to expel me and to pay so dearly for the overwhelming anxieties and the evils which result from war?

If wild animals hated me in this manner, I would be re-
signed and I would place the blame on nature which inflicted this violent character on them. If I were hated by unreasoning animals I would attribute their hatred to their
ignorance, saying that they are too lacking in intelligence
to be capable of grasping the advantages that I offer them.
But alas! O infamous and monstrous disgrace! God has created only one animal that is endowed with reason — man!
Only one, alas, who is able to conceive the idea of God! He

alone nature has made sensible of good will and harmony, and yet I can more easily find sanctuary among wild animals than among men.

Behold the heavenly spheres: although having neither the same movement nor the same functions, they nonetheless reveal, in their uniformity and for incalculable centuries, a steady harmony. The elements, although in an incessant battle against one another, nonetheless are maintained, in the midst of so much discord, by their own strength in constant equilibrium. And does there not exist a permanent accord among the members of a living body? What a painful readiness to protect one another! And is there anything more dissimilar than body and soul? And yet it is in their separation that they demonstrate how intimately nature has bound them together! And just as life is nothing but the union of the body and the soul, health, in turn, is only the state resulting from a remarkable harmony among all the functions of the organism.

Animals, deprived of the faculty of reasoning, live together on good terms, each grouped according to its species as is proper for peaceful citizens. Elephants live in herds, sheep are pastured together. Cranes and jays fly in flocks. Storks, which teach piety and goodness, hold their councils. Dolphins protect one another, performing mutual services. As for the ants and the bees, the organization and good understanding that reign among these insects are universally known. But why stress these animals which, lacking reason, at least have their senses? Even trees and plants show signs of friendship! The vine embraces the young elm and the peach tree loves the vine. Even things without any feeling seem to enjoy the benefit of peace. Though lacking in the faculty of feeling, they nonetheless possess — because they have continuance — affinities with everything that feels. Is there anything more unfeeling than stone? Yet in observing it, one would say that it contains within itself the idea of peace and harmony. Thus the magnet attracts the iron and, having attracted it, holds it.

This faculty of attraction is also displayed among the wild beasts. However ferocious they may be, lions never fight among themselves. The wild boar never attacks another wild boar with its deadly tooth. The lynx lives at peace with his kind. The dragon does not attack the dragon. As for the good will among wolves, it has become proverbial. I may add a still more surprising example: the evil spirits, who were the first to break the peace between God and men, and who since then have never ceased their work of destruction, are united among themselves and always in agreement when its enforcement is concerned.

Men alone, who should be most inclined to the union of which they have so great a need, remain deaf to the voice of nature, although it is so communicative and so efficacious elsewhere. Their reunions do not unite them. The great advantages that would result from their agreement mean nothing to them and cannot attach them to one another. An awareness of the evils that result from war and their sad experience of it are without the slightest influence on them.

And yet everything seems to invite them to peace: their appearance, which is common to all men; their voice, which is the gift of all — while other species of animals differ among themselves according to the shape of their bodies. Besides, men alone possess the faculty of reasoning, which is the same for each, in which they differ completely from other creatures. Man alone possesses the gift of words, that great conciliator of friendship. Nature has also placed in each the seed of virtue and of all knowledge. It has endowed human beings with a tender and gentle character which leads men toward good will for their neighbor and grants them the delight of making themselves loved, as well as with the pleasure of making themselves useful to one another, unless, corrupted by evil passions, they degenerate like the victims of Circe[2] and become wild beasts. Apparently it is as a result of man's moral nature that we commonly call *humane* everything that applies to the good will which individuals practice toward each other. So the term *humanity* does not reveal the physical man but his morals, morals which are worthy of nature. Finally, nature has granted him tears, the irrefragable proof of his sensitivity, which lead men to forgive and to forget offenses which may hurt them and which, like a veil, darken the serenity of friendship.

Observe, therefore, in how many ways nature tried to teach you harmony! She was not satisfied, however, with making friendship pleasant simply for the charm of mutual benevolence; she wanted this feeling to be indispensable as well. It is for this reason that she so arranged it that, by their very nature and their faculties, man's body and spirit cannot get along without the help of other men, however humble they may be. It is in order that this inequality should be compensated for by reciprocal services that nature has not given the same gifts to all and has not distributed them in an equal manner. She has not endowed different regions with the same products so that necessity would force men into commerce which would thus lead them toward friendship for each other. This same nature provided animals with natural weapons for defense so that each might watch out for his individual security. But she created one animal, man, unarmed and weak, so that he could insure his safety only by union with his fellows and by reciprocal assistance. Yes, necessity created societies[3] and taught men to unite that they might guard their common defense against brigands or other forces which attack them by violence.

Indeed, the circumstances and conditions of life are such that man can never suffice unto himself. The human race would have perished at its very beginning if conjugal union had not propagated the species. Man is scarcely born before he is on the point of leaving life; he would lose it at the very threshold of his existence if the practiced hand of the midwife and the tender cares of the nurse did not come to his aid. Nature[4] seems to have sown in the heart of parents this powerful and intense spark of tenderness which makes them love their children even before they are born. Let us consider, too, the tenderness of children for parents, whose infirmities and age are alleviated by the care which in turn they are given. Finally, let us add to all that the bonds of relationship and friendship. Indeed, there exist among certain men powerful affinities because of the similarities of their natures, their inclinations and their tastes, and their physical traits. These affinities induce mutual benevolence. And how many people experience the irresistible power of a secret appeal of the soul which impels and urges them toward a profound reciprocal sympathy! The ancients, who were amazed by it, attributed this admirable emotion to divine power and to the good spirits who urge human beings on to love and mutual affection.

Thus, in every way, nature teaches peace and harmony; so many attractions engage us to love them! Nature offers us so many bonds to attach us to them! And so many reasons urge us to preserve them! After all that, let someone tell us who is the demon capable of destroying, who is the evil spirit who — shattering, breaking, dividing everything — creates in the heart of men this insatiable rage for war? Who, I wonder — without the habit and the indolence that rob us of our faculty for surprise and even the awareness of evil — who could believe that these men who argue, who quarrel, who fight with such tenacity, are still possessed of reason? They pillage, they kill, they shed floods of human blood, they ruin absolutely everything, sacred and profane. There is no treaty of friendship so firm, no alliance so strong, or sacred, that they do not attempt to break it at the cost of their own ruin. But is it necessary to add that the common denomination of *man* should suffice to make mortals live on good terms?

Nonetheless, grant that nature, which can do everything with animals, can do nothing with men. But are the teachings of Christ then without effect on Christians? If it is possible that the teachings of nature, so influential on unreasoning animals, are of slight effect on men, is it not surprising that the Christian doctrine, whose superiority of precepts outweighs those of nature, cannot induce men to recognize boldly what it preaches above everything else: namely, peace and mutual assistance? Why, then, does it not unlearn men of this ungodly and ferocious dementia of making war on each other?

When I hear a man's voice, I hasten toward him as toward the animal whom a common birth has made my fellow; I hope to find near him a little place where I can rest. When I hear the name of Christians, I hurry even with more eagerness, as toward those who give me the hope of living at liberty with them. But — O height of grief! — here too, I am ashamed to confess, the tribunals, the royal courts, the senates, the temples, the public places, resound with such disputes and quarrels as were never seen among the pagans. So that the crowd of lawyers, to whom we owe in great part the misfortunes of men, passes unnoticed here — so vast is the number of wranglers!

I see a city, and at once hope is reborn in my soul; here at least, I tell myself, good understanding rules among men. How could it be otherwise? They are surrounded by the same walls, they are governed by the same laws and — like passengers on the same ship — are exposed to the same dangers. But — poor me! — here too all is divided by discord, to such a point that I cannot find in the whole city a single house where I can rest.

I put aside, for the moment, the common people who, like a wild sea, are either in constant, reasonless agitation, or else are passive, letting themselves be borne by the waves. It is the palace of the princes that I enter as into a sure refuge. Peace, I say to myself, no doubt reigns in this place; for are not the great wiser than the common people? Have they not been *chosen* to govern[5] precisely because of their wisdom and their gift of foresight? And is it not their mission, not only to watch over the destiny of the teachings of him who is the Master and the Prince of Peace, who loves me and offers me to all, but also — since he recommends me to their particular care — to implant me in the bosom of their empires? So that, in truth, everything at first seems to be of good augury. On seeing me, they welcome me with cordiality and in the nicest way in the world. I see men embrace each other and meet at banquets to eat and drink joyously. In short, they perform all the duties incumbent on men living in society. But — what an indignity! — on looking closer, I see that, in reality, one cannot discover among them the slightest shadow of real harmony. All is lies and falsity. Basically, everything and everyone is disunited. Whether exposed in the light of day or hidden in the shadows of their hearts, discord and corruption rule as masters. So it was even less possible to discover among the powerful a little corner where I could install myself, because they themselves are the essential cause of all the dissensions and of every war that ravages humanity.

Unhappy me! After so many disappointments and endless disillusionments, where shall I turn? The princes, I said then, are illustrious rather for their position than for their knowledge. They are guided by their passions rather than by their reason. Therefore, I will take refuge with the scholars. Sciences and letters surely make them men in all the meaning of this term; doubtless, philosophy makes them supermen and theology makes them divine. At last I will find among these chosen people a sure and certain repose. But alas, inconceivable grief! Here too war reigns, the all-powerful master; a war which, for being less cruel, is only the more foolish. One school is fighting with another, as though immutable truth would vary according to place. Certain truths approved by one do not cross the sea. Certain others scale the Alps. Still others cannot go beyond the Rhine. And that is not all! Within a single academy, the rhetorician fights the dialectician, the theologian is the enemy of the legist. Even in the same science, in the same domain, Scottist fights Thomist; Nominalist is at war with Realist; the Peripatetics wrangle with the Platonists — to such a point that they never agree on the slightest point[6]. Their disputes arise over inconceivably futile and abstract matters, to such a degree that the violence of the arguments leads to insult, and insult to blows. Thus, although the question is not decided with deadly weapons, they nonetheless drag each other in the mud, violently exchanging venomous words, each one darting his tongue in a mortal hit at the expense of the good name of his adversary.

Betrayed and neglected by all, I wonder where I can turn now? Religion remains my last refuge. It appears to my hope like an anchor of safety; its exercise is common to all believers although each one practices it in his own manner, differentiated by the rites and practices of their cults — that is, by those ceremonies which are intrusted to those commonly called priests.

Observing Christian priests from a distance, the hope of finding a sure refuge among them rises in me. Their white habits decorated with parti-colored embroidery appeal to me. I perceive the sign of the cross which is the symbol of peace. I hear them call one another by the sweet name of *brother*, which serves as a proof of the perfect love that unites them. I hear their greetings of peace which foretell happiness. I see that they have everything in common: the same college of priests, the same temple, the same rules, the same place of daily gatherings. Who would not agree that peace has found its place here? But — O height of misery! — there is not a college which lives on good terms with its bishop! Even that would be of little importance, if the priests at least were not torn among themselves by internal struggles. Is there a single one who has not a motive for disputing with his colleague? Paul would not permit a Christian to be at variance with another Christian. But here a priest takes a stand against another priest, a bishop against a bishop! However, some people inclined to be indulgent will say: In spite of all that, cannot we excuse them to some extent? For through long habit they have become like the profane. For example, inspired by the profane, they have so long owned lands that they doubtless believe that they are authorized in asserting their rights of seniority against each other when they claim these domains as their property.

However, there remains one class of men so attached to religion that, even if they so desired, they could no more separate themselves from it than a turtle could separate itself from its shell — the monks. I might easily have hoped to find a safe place among the latter if so many disappointed hopes had not taught me not to hope. And yet, that I might not reproach myself with not having tried everything, I took the chance. Do you want to know the result? I stayed nowhere a shorter time than with them. Was there anything to hope, I ask, where religion is in conflict with itself? They are divided into as many factions as there are brotherhoods. The Dominicans are at drawn swords with the barefooted Franciscans, the Benedictines with the Bernardines. There are as many cults as there are names, and consequently as many different ceremonies, for fear, doubtless, of agreeing on anything whatsoever; each brotherhood honors and worships only its own rites and its own rules, while it curses and execrates those of its "rivals." Even united in common council, one sees them split into opposing factions: the Franciscans hate the Celestins, and both despise the *Conventuals,* those whose name is taken from the word *convent,* although even among themselves none of them can *convene* peacefully.[7]

It will be easily understood that, after having learned that I had nothing to hope here, I wanted to withdraw into some obscure little monastery where, among hermits forgotten by the world, I might taste real calm. But — I confess it with sorrow, even while hoping that I am mistaken — up to now I have discovered none that were not corrupted by hatred and internal strife. I feel ashamed to relate what stormy quarrels these ferocious old men, so imposing with their beards and their attire, stir up for the most trifling things. But they impose on themselves infinitely more, by regarding themselves as great scholars and great saints.

And one day hope suggested that among so many human beings closely united by bonds of marriage, there would at last be granted me a little retreat under the roof of a peaceful couple. How promising was the appearance of these peaceful people, living between the same walls, sharing their property in common, sharing the same bed, and having children together! Not to speak of the fact that their mutual rights to their bodies must make of the two a single being. But here again penetrated that impious Eris,[8] to sow discord in souls attached by so many bonds. In spite of that, I would prefer a place among these humble people rather than among those who, in decking themselves with so many pompous titles, with so many external distinctions, and surrounding themselves with so many ceremonials, do not cease praising themselves — and wrongly, alas! — for practicing in regard to their fellowmen the most absolute so-called charity.

Finally, there remained only the hope that I might manage at least to find a place in the heart of some man — just one! But even this hope I had to abandon quickly. For man, alone as he is, is still at war with himself. His reason is at war with his affections, while his affections, left to themselves, are in perpetual conflict among themselves; modesty or godliness pull him in one direction, cupidity hauls him in the other. Besides, passions sway him: lust, anger, ambition, greediness, each govern the man as it will.

In spite of this, and while letting themselves be dominated by passions, these same men are yet not ashamed to arrogate to themselves the title of Christians — they who cannot even agree on the most worthy thing which the nature of Christ offers, on what is his very own, and what evolves from his doctrine and his life.

II

When one considers the whole life of Jesus, indeed, what is it if not an uninterrupted lesson in peace and mutual love? Do his precepts and his parables teach anything but harmony and mutual assistance among men?[9] When the noble prophet Isaiah, divinely inspired, announced the coming of the Messiah, the reconciler of all things here below, did he predict a violent satrap, a destroyer of cities, a warrior, a conqueror? Certainly not! No! Then what was his message? He announced the "Prince of Peace" (Isaiah 9:6). And when he wanted to make us understand the nature of the most charming of princes, he described it by the attribute that seemed to him the most remarkable and the most appropriate to his character — peace. This conception of Isaiah (52:7) is not surprising. He thought the same as the pagan poet Silius, who in eulogistic terms had said of me: "Peace is the best thing nature has granted to men." And David, that mystical player of the zither, was of the same opinion as Isaiah when he sang: "The place of God and his dwelling are in peace, they are not under tents nor in the fields. . . . He is a Prince of Peace, he loves peace, discord offends him."

Elsewhere, Isaiah calls peace "the work of righteousness" (Isaiah 32:17). He thinks, if I am not mistaken, the same as Paul, after the latter was transformed from Saul the fanatic into the most pacific man preaching peace. And, preferring mutual love to all the other gifts of the Holy Spirit, he made my praise ring in the ears of the Corinthians with great eloquence and with a courage worthy of the highest commendation. Could I not be proud that so venerated a man praised me? This same Paul speaks in certain places of the "Peace of God" (Colossians 3:15), in others of the "God of Peace" (Hebrews 13:20), thus making evident the truth that these two notions are so inseparable that peace can hardly prosper where God is not, and that God cannot be found in a place where peace is not. The Bible also speaks to us of ministers of God whom it calls angels or "Ambassadors of Peace" (Isaiah 33:7), so that it is easy to conclude by what name are to be called those who must be considered as "Ambassadors of War."

Hear me then, valiant warriors, and look closely at the banner under which you are fighting. You are fighting under the flag of him who first sowed discord between God and man. All the evils from which humanity suffers are a result of this discord.

There is nothing more frivolous or less justified than the arguments of those who claim that in Holy Scripture there is a question of a God of armies and a God of vengeance. There is a great difference between God as the Jews conceive him and the God of the Christians, although, in essence, the same God is concerned in both. But since these ancient concepts do not displease you, let us admit that there exists a God of armies, so long as one understands by army the mobilization of *all the virtues* under whose protection men fight *all the vices.* Let us admit, too, that there exists a God of vengeance. But only if one understands by vengeance the punishment of vices, such as those cruel massacres with which the books of the Jews abound, aimed not at the annihilation of innocent men, but at the destruction in their hearts of guilty passions. I even add — in order to be able to develop more amply what I have said — that when Holy Scripture wishes to express absolute happiness, it does so by the word "Peace." Thus Isaiah said: "My people shall dwell in a peaceable habitation" (Isaiah 32:18). And elsewhere: "Peace shall be upon Israel" (Psalms 125:5). Also Isaiah holds in great esteem those who proclaim peace and happy events.

All those who predicted the Messiah heralded peace. On

the other hand, all those who heralded war proclaimed what is most opposed to the nature of Christ. What was the goal for which the Son of God came down to earth if not the desire to reconcile God and the world, so that men might be united among themselves by a mutual and indestructible love, and to make man his friend? He was sent on earth to be my ambassador and my missionary. That is why he wanted Solomon, whose name in our language means peace, to be his image on earth. How great was David! And yet, because he had been a warrior, and because he was stained with human blood, he had not made himself worthy of building the house of God or of reflecting the image of the Messiah, the Peaceful.

Let that serve you as a warning, impetuous warrior! If even the wars undertaken at the order of God soil and degrade men, think of the effect of those which are unleashed by the ambition, anger, and passions of man!

If the fact of shedding pagan blood is of such a nature as to dishonor a Christian prince, let us reflect on the consequences of this immense shedding of Christian blood. I implore you, O Christian Prince, if you are really such, to look upon the image of our Lord, your prince. Consider how he entered his kingdom, how he left it, how he died, and you will at once understand how you must govern your own so that your first and last care will be only for peace and harmony.

When Christ was born, did the angels sound trumpets and drums? The Hebrews, who were permitted to wage war, well understood the loud sound of trumpets. They were warnings well suited to those whose religion permitted them to hate the enemy. But the angels, missionaries of peace, made a different song ring out to the peaceful race. Did they give a signal for war? Did they promise victories, triumphs, and trophies? Not at all! What then did they announce? In harmony with the oracles of the prophets, they proclaimed peace, and they announced it, not to those who long only for murder and battle, nor to those who are transported with joy at the idea of taking up arms, but to those who, of their own good will, are inclined to peace and harmony. Let men make what claims they will to excuse their passion for war; if they did not like it, they would not live in continual conflict; they would not set upon one another with such mortal hatred.

And yet what was it that Jesus, scarcely emerged from infancy, taught, if it was not peace? He was accustomed to greet his fellows in these terms: "Peace be unto you!" (Luke 24:36), and he made of this formula the customary expression which his disciples used to greet one another — the only phrase worthy of the Christian name. The apostles did not forget this salutation; they began their letters by the wish for peace, and this wish remains the object of the aspiration of all those who aim at salvation. He who wishes for health desires an excellent thing. But the man who ardently asks for peace asks at the same time for the most perfect happiness.

It is peace that Christ preached to his people during his whole life. Do you want me to recall how he addressed his followers at the moment of his death? "Love one another, as I have loved you" (John 15:12). And again: "My peace I give unto you; peace I leave with you" (John 14:27). Do you hear what he left his followers at the last moments of his existence? Was it horses? warriors? riches? the right to command people? None of that! What then did he bequeath them? He bequeathed them peace! Peace among friends, peace among enemies.

Let us recall and weigh in our spirit the words which, after the Last Supper, on the very threshold of death, Jesus addressed to the Almighty Father. The object of his prayer was, in my opinion, far from being banal or vulgar, when he knew that whatever he asked would be granted him. "Holy Father," he prayed, "keep them through thine own name that they may be one as we are" (John 17:11). Such was the union which Jesus required of his disciples. He did not say, "that they may be unanimous," but he said, "that they may be one." And that not in *any* manner, but "as we are one" — that is, in the most perfect and ineffable manner. And all that to show them that mortals cannot possibly live in security and happiness if they do not maintain mutual peace.

The great of this world supply their subjects with special insignia so that they may be recognized, especially in war, where they can be distinguished from their adversaries. Well, the mark that distinguishes the disciples of Christ is only reciprocal love. "By this," he said, "that shall all men know that you are my disciples. They will not know you according to your apparel, nor according to your nourishment, nor according to your fasts nor even according to the number of prayers and psalms that you recite. They will know you only by the fact that you love one another. And that, not in any manner, but as I myself have loved you" (John 13:35, 34). "Many are the precepts of the philosophers," he said again. "Infinitely varied are the laws of Moses. The edicts of kings are not less many or less varied. I give you only one commandment: it is that you love one another."

Also, when Jesus gave his young disciples a formula for prayer, he attracted attention admirably to the necessity of universal harmony: "Our Father," he said. "The prayer is by one, but the request is for all. They are all of *one* family, they form *one* house, they depend on *one* Father." How then can they agree in thinking that they can be divided and fight among themselves? With what name will you call upon the common Father of all men when you draw your sword against your own brother? It is because Jesus wanted this single commandment to sink deep in the hearts of his disciples that he inculcated in them by so many symbols, so many parables and precepts, the love of peace.

Jesus called himself a shepherd, and he called his disciples his sheep; but what must the wolves do if the sheep destroy each other? When he calls himself a vine and his disciples the branches, does he express anything but solidarity? How monstrous to see one branch of a vine fight with another branch! Would it not be equally so to see a Christian fight with a Christian? Finally, if there is any truth worthy of the veneration of Christians, and if they ought to consider it as the most sacred object and most worthy of attention, is it not those words, which, in his last moments, Jesus transmitted like a testament to his children, in recommending that they never forget them? But what did he teach them at this last moment, what did he command them? Was it not to love one another?

What is the meaning of the communion with the body and blood of Christ if not a new confirmation of the close and indestructible union which should exist among men? As he knew that peace cannot be consolidated where men argue over glory, honor, and riches, he extirpated radically from the soul of his disciples all passion of that nature. He ordered them to do good unto those who harmed them. In spite of all that, these princes who, for the most trifling injuries, destroy the world from top to bottom and throw a great part of humanity into war, pass for Christians.

Jesus taught that he who wishes to be the prince of his people must at the same time be the benefactor, and not dominate his subjects otherwise than by making himself the best of them and the most useful to all. In spite of that, there are princes who are not ashamed to cause the greatest ruin for the mere purpose of enlarging the territory of their realm. Jesus taught his disciples to live from day to day like the birds and the flowers; not to worry about tomorrow and to place all their hope in Heaven. He excluded the rich from the heavenly kingdom. That does not in the least prevent princes from shedding torrents of blood for some amount of money that was not turned over to them on time or which was not even owed to them! There are causes for war, it must be admitted, which seem to be perfectly "just." But is this behavior in the spirit of Christ, of him who, setting himself as an example for his disciples, recommended to them his own gentle and peaceful nature? He ordered them to leave the offering on the altar and not to consecrate it to him until they were reconciled with their fellow-men. What does that mean if not that it is the duty of men to prefer harmony and peace to everything else, and that any sacrifice which is not offered under the seal of peace is repulsive to God? God, as the Jews conceive him, refuses the offering, whether it is a sheep or a goat, when those who offer it are in conflict with one another. Yet Christians, while massacring each other in war, do not hesitate to offer God human sacrifices.

Do you remember the symbol of harmony which Jesus gives us in the image of a hen who, gathering her little ones under her wings, makes one with them? Like her, he is the protector, gathering men, by his exhortations, into a whole. How does it happen then that these men are so rapacious and insatiable? But that is not all: Jesus is the cornerstone that joins the walls and upholds them. How is it possible then for his vicars to stir up the whole world to war and arouse nation against nation? What! They have as their Prince him who was the most sublime conciliator, and they are incapable of establishing harmony among themselves? And Christ, who reconciled Pilate and Herod, has no power to lead his own to peace? In the last hours of his life, Jesus blamed the attitude of Peter, then still half Jew, because he prepared to defend him against his aggressors, sword in hand. And he ordered him to put it back in its scabbard. After that, they dare call Christian him who holds the sword always raised and thrusts it into the flank of another Christian for the most trifling reasons? Could he, who in dying prayed for his executioners, have endured to be defended in this fashion?

All the holy books, whether in the Old Testament or the New, speak only of peace and understanding, while the life of Christians is only a tissue of intrigues and massacres. Who can explain whence comes this more than savage barbarity, that so many sublime examples can neither overcome nor mitigate?

Let Christians decide at last to follow the doctrine of Christ and live in the peace it teaches — or let them cease to glorify themselves with the name of Christians! Oh, how long will their life refute the beauty of their name? Ornament as they will their garments and their churches with the sign of the cross, Jesus will not recognize it as the symbol of peace; he will not recognize it so long as their actions refute it. United at the moment when they saw him ascend into Heaven, they must still be united to receive the Holy Spirit. He promised to be among those always who were united, so that no man might hope to find him there where they fought one another.

What does that ardent spirit, the human soul itself, mean, if not love? The soul communicates itself like fire, which spreads and propagates infinitely without consuming itself. Do you now want proof that this soul itself is subject to peace? Listen and judge: "They are all," said Jesus of his disciples, "of one heart and of one soul" (Acts 4:32). Separate the soul from the body and at once all the members, which the soul retained in perfect harmony, perish. Remove peace from society; the latter will break up and Christian life will perish with it.

Theologians claim that by the communion of the sacraments the heavenly spirit is communicated to the believer. Are they telling the truth? If so, then what is the effect of this heavenly spirit? I mean, where is the harmony which should reign among men who are all "of one heart and of one soul"? Or are they telling us stories? If that is so, why do they grant so many honors to things which are only stories? I say this, not to steal anything from the beauty of the sacraments, but only to force Christians to blush the more for their actions.

The Christian people are called a Church — *Ecclesia*. To what does this denomination exhort us if not to mutual understanding? Is there anything in common between a military camp and a Church? The latter means indestructible union; the military camp is the embodiment of murderous discord. If you pride yourself on being a part of the Church, what have you in common with war? If, on the other hand, you have strayed from it, what is there in common between you and Jesus? If you have all the same earthly dwelling, if you are governed by the same Prince, if you all obey the same laws, if you are all initiates of the same sacraments, if you receive the same recompense and expect the same reward, how can there be so many disorders and divisions among you? We see these ungodly companions in arms, led and paid to practice murder and brigandage, agree perfectly among themselves, simply because they kill and pillage under the same flag. And so many spiritual bonds are without any effect to unite you who profess to be Christians!

Can it be that so many sacraments exert not the slightest effect upon you? Baptism is common to all. Because of that we are reborn in Christ, and beyond this world we are incorporated in the body of Christ. But is there anything more harmonious than the members of a single body? After baptism, none is free — neither slave, nor barbarian, nor Greek, nor man, nor woman; all are men in Christ who brings all into harmony. The Scythians are so strongly bound to one another by a few drops of blood which they drink from the same cup that they do not hesitate at any sacrifice, and go so far as to risk death to serve their friends. Friendship is not less honored among the pagans; a meal in common suffices to consolidate it. Yet neither the blessed bread nor the sacred cup can keep Christians friendly, in that same friendship which Jesus himself made inviolable and which masses constantly renew and represent. If Jesus wasted his suffering and his time, what is the use of all these ceremonies today? If he accomplished something really worthy of our praise and of our attention, why do you disdain his work as though it were something contemptible and ridiculous?

How can he dare to approach the communion table, which is the symbol of friendship, or to take part in the repast of peace, he who makes war against his fellow men and prepares to destroy those for whose redemption Jesus died; how dare he, who is ready to shed the blood of those for whom Christ shed his own blood? O hard hearts that nothing can move! Union reigns among so many things — but the life of man is filled with so many inconceivable divisions. And yet these men are subject to the same laws: the same birth, the same necessity to grow old, the same inevitable death. They all come from the same Heavenly Father, all believe in the same God. They are all redeemed by the same blood, all initiated in the same cult, they all partake in the same sacraments; the gifts, favors, which rain upon them come from the same source and are common to all. The same Church is common to all, the same advantages are offered for the enjoyment of each one. The famous city of Jerusalem, which so many Christians aspire to visit, takes its name from the concept of peace of which it is the symbol. The role of the Church is to illustrate this symbol, which is that of harmony among men.[10] But how does it happen that it differs thus radically from what was its first model? Can it be that neither ingenious nature, with its immense resources, nor Jesus himself, with his sublime precepts and his many symbols and mysteries, are of any help in establishing peace among men? Is the dictum then true that claims that ill deeds unite the wicked in friendship, but that only Christians are unable to be reconciled among themselves, either by evil or by good?

III

Is there anything more fragile and more brief than human life? To how many sicknesses and ills it is subject! And though it is sown with far more sorrows than men can endure, their inconsequence and their aberration inevitably produce even more painful ones. They behave with such furious intolerance that they destroy and violate the sublime bonds of nature and the sacred bonds of Jesus. They respect no signed treaty. They make war at all times, in all places, without a purpose, and without end. Nations against nations, cities against cities, parties against parties, princes against princes. For the stupidity or the ambition of two mortal wretches, both subject, from one moment to another, to the same inflexible death, the natural order of things is destroyed from top to bottom.

I pass silently over the tragedies of ancient wars. I will stress only those which have taken place in the course of these last years. Where is the land or the sea where people have not fought in the most cruel manner? Where is the river that has not been dyed with human blood, the region that has not been watered with Christian blood? O supreme shame! They behave more cruelly in battle than non-Christians, more savagely than wild beasts.

No wars undertaken by Christian peoples should be supported except against vice. But unhappily, the Christians have identified themselves with vices, and men wage pitiless war against men. The Jews did not go to war except on the express orders of God. But the Christians, if we put aside the pretexts invoked and examine things at all carefully, are driven to war by ambition, they are led by furious intolerance, they let themselves be carried away by the most insatiable greediness. And that is not all. The Jews nearly always fought against foreign infidels alone, while the Christians live at peace with the Turk but fight all the harder among themselves. When the tyrants of the past devoted themselves to bloody battles, they were motivated by a thirst for glory. But in enslaving foreign and barbarous nations, they were often guided by the desire to be useful to the vanquished, and, though conquerors, they tried to make them grateful. They took care that the victory should be as bloodless as possible so that real glory might be the price of their triumph, and their magnanimity would be the consolation of the vanquished.

One blushes to recall the shameful and frivolous motives for which Christian potentates take up arms against people. One proves or forges some antiquated right as though it were of the slightest importance that one prince or another should govern the state so long as public interests are well administered. Another takes as his pretext a point omitted from a treaty with innumerable clauses.[11] A third attacks a fourth because of a promised bride who was refused him or taken from him, or because of too free a joke. And the height of such infamies is that there are princes who, aware that their authority is weakening as a result — so they believe — of too long a peace, because it has enabled their subjects to become too closely united, secretly and diabolically agree with other princes so that, when a pretext can be found at last, they will provoke a war. This war would be designed solely to divide by discord those who, up to now, have lived closely united and — after having roused them against each other, and because of the arbitrary and unchecked authority which war gives — to despoil the unfortunate people. That is what vicious princes watch for, to assuage their unhealthy passions at the cost of evil to innocent people and, in times of peace, to neglect totally their duties toward the state.

From what hell does that demon come who succeeds in

injecting this poison into the hearts of Christians? Who taught them this tyranny that the Dionysius, Mezence, and Phalaris[12] themselves never attained? They are wild beasts rather than men, noble only to the extent that tyranny can make them noble. They have never united except to do evil, and they are never in agreement except to oppress their peoples. And those who behave in this way are regarded as Christians! And thus stained with blood, do they dare — shall they be permitted — to enter the churches and approach the altars? They are the scourge of nations and deserve to be deported to the farthest islands of the world. If, as they claim, they are members of one Christian body, why should not each be glad at the happiness of the other?

In our times, the proximity of a somewhat too flourishing country is almost a legitimate motive for war. Indeed, if we want to be just and speak clearly, what other cause has impelled and still impels so many people to take up arms against France, if not the fact that this is the most flourishing country of all? No country in Europe possesses a vaster expanse. Nowhere is the Senate more august, the Academy more illustrious. No country enjoys more harmony than the French people, and for that very reason, more power in the world. Nowhere are laws better applied and, as far as religion is concerned, nowhere has the integrity of the doctrine been more respected than in France. It is neither corrupted by commerce, as with the Italians, nor poisoned by the proximity of the Turks and the Moors, as with the Hungarians and the Spanish, while Germany, to say nothing of Bohemia, is divided into a host of kingdoms, and, in spite of the number of petty kings, there is not a shadow of authority. Only in France, intact flower of the kingdom of Christ, is his sanctuary the surest.

Well, if by chance any storm comes up, France will be attacked in every way, assailed by all the tricks of those who desire her ruin for the sole pleasure of the devastation that they will have caused. After that, can we say that these men possess the slightest fragment of the Christian spirit? For — I repeat — in spite of such infamous practices, these gentlemen invoke the Christian religion and even claim that they are extending the empire of Christ by such means! What a cruel monstrosity to believe that one is never of such use to the Christian cause as when destroying from top to bottom the most beautiful and the most flourishing part of the kingdom of Christ!

What can be said of all this except that these people surpass by their violence the most ferocious animals? Wild beasts do not fight among themselves, and when a struggle does take place, it does not occur among animals of the same species. I have already said it and I repeat it, in order to stamp it better on the memory of those who hear me. The snake does not attack the snake, the lynx lives on good terms with the lynx. On the other hand, when these animals do tear each other to pieces, they do it with their own means, nature having endowed them with natural weapons, while men were born unarmed. But — good God! — what terrible weapons anger has forged for them![13] They assail one another with infernal machines. What uninformed being could ever believe that cannons are a human invention? Besides, when wild animals attack each other, they are not in such great numbers. Have ten lions ever been seen to attack ten bulls? On the other hand, how often have twenty thousand Christians been seen to attack twenty thousand others, to settle their differences by steel, all equally eager to destroy their brothers and to shed their blood! Wild beasts do not make war unless hunger or the protection of their little ones forces them to do so. But seek the reasons that drive Christians to take up arms; there is no injury, however insignificant it may be, which does not seem to them a sufficient pretext to start a war.

If the common people were guilty of such a folly, they

would be excused on a pretext of their ignorance; if young people, their inexperience would be invoked; if the profane were guilty, their quality would make the atrocity of the act less horrible. But unfortunately, we see that most wars spring from the will of those whose example and moderation ought to be most proper for calming the unrest of the people.

The people, so despised and so obscure, found and build magnificent cities, administer them, enrich them by their labor, and embellish them by their efforts. The despots slip in furtively and, like wasps stealing honey which has been gathered with so much trouble by a swarm of bees, they pillage, break, and destroy in the most pitiless manner what was amassed and constructed with so much trouble by a whole people.

Let him who has lost the memory of ancient wars appeal to his recollection and recall those of the past dozen years. Let him seek the cause. He will find that all were undertaken at the caprice of princes to the great detriment of the people whom these wars in no way concerned. What was formerly shameful among pagans — that old men covered their white hairs with a war helmet — is now considered among Christians as a perfectly honorable thing. Nason found it shameful that an old man should be a soldier.[14] But today, a septuagenarian warrior seems to us a magnificent being.

The clergy itself is not ashamed to fight, these same theologians, whom God never permitted — any more than did the law of Moses, hard as it was — to stain themselves with blood. Yes, these theologians, who teach the religion of Christ, are not ashamed to fight! Bishops, cardinals, popes, who are vicars of Christ — none among them is ashamed to start the war that Jesus so execrated. What is there in common between the helmet and the miter? What relation between the crosier and the sword, between the holy book of the Gospel and the shield? What harmony is there between the sign of peace with which people greet each other and the fact of driving violently a whole world into the most bloody struggle? Is it not preaching peace in words and preparing for war in deeds? Is it not preaching war with the same mouth with which one preaches the pacific doctrines of Christ, and praising with the same voice both God and Satan? Is it not stirring up simple people to war and murder at the very moment when they come to church to hear from such lips the gospel teachings?

Bishop, how dare you, who hold the place of the Apostles, teach people things that touch on war at the same time that you teach them the precepts of these Apostles? You need not fear that they will answer you with those words of Isaiah to the messengers of the Messiah: "How beautiful are the feet of him that bringeth good tidings, that publisheth peace, that publisheth salvation" (Isaiah 52:7). Let us reverse, on hearing you, the meaning of this thought and it would become: "How frightful is the tongue of priests who exhort to war, who stir up evil, who lead us into temptation to kill."

The religion of the Romans, however pagan they may have been, forced every Roman who entered the house of the grand priest to swear that he would keep his hand pure of all shedding of blood to the point even of renouncing vengeance if he were wounded. Emperor Titus Vespasian, a pagan, remained faithful to this vow, and he was showered with praise for it and celebrated by a famous writer of his country. But today all modesty has disappeared. Among Christians, it is the priests dedicated to God, and the monks, claiming in some way to be more accomplished than the priests, who inflame and excite us to murder and massacre, princes as well as peoples. Of the trumpet of the Gospel they have made a trumpet of war. Forgetful of their dignity, they run tirelessly in all directions, arranging all sorts of maneuvers, enduring all imaginable fatigue so long as they succeed in bringing about war. And the princes themselves, who, without the stimulus of the clergy, perhaps would not break the peace and whose duty it would be to use their authority to calm the tempest of passions, are led to war by these servants of God. Still, the most astonishing thing is that the priests fight among themselves, and for things for which the wise men of antiquity had nothing but scorn, and which should be disdained especially by those who have taken the succession of the Apostles.

Several years ago, when a disastrous misfortune led the world to war, certain evangelical preachers — the Minorites and the Dominicans —thundered from the sacred pulpit, stirring up with all their strength the fury of those who were already inclined to war. They aroused one against another, first the English and then the French. All of them encouraged war, none advised peace, except one or two who, for having pronounced my name, were threatened with death.

We witnessed then the sinister spectacle offered by bishops and cardinals[15] who, forgetful of their position, ran about, using all their strength to add poison to the common evil with which all were already afflicted. They called on Pope Julius II and on the kings, urging them to hasten the war, as though they had not been mad enough themselves. At the same time they strove to find magnificent pretexts to justify these acts of folly. Sometimes it was laws handed down by our ancestors, sometimes the teachings of the fathers of the Church. They went so far as to twist the meaning of the words of Holy Scripture — and did it without the slightest scruple, not to say sacrilegiously. And here is where things stand at present. Nothing is more imprudent or more unrighteous than to protest against war, than to praise what Jesus, with his own mouth, praised above all things. Thus any man who urges peace (that is to say, the most salutary thing), any man who wants to turn his country away from war (which is the worst thing), is regarded as a bad patriot who reveals little interest in the happiness of his people and little devotion to his king.

In our times, the spectacle is offered of priests who follow the army, of bishops with their whole suites abandoning their churches, to put themselves at the service of the war. But what is much worse is that war makes priests! War makes bishops! War makes cardinals! The latter bear the title of Legate of War and are considered worthy successors of the Apostles.[16] And that is not surprising: like true children of Mars they desire nothing but war. Finally, to make this evil completely incurable, they cover this great sacrilege with the pretext of piety; their flags bear the sign of the cross. The sinister mercenaries, paid to practice murder and brigandage, bear the cross before them! Thus the cross, which alone could have argued against war, becomes the symbol of war.

What have you in common with the cross, nefarious warrior, whose character and acts make you resemble dragons, tigers, and wolves? The cross belongs to him who won the victory, not by killing, but by giving his own life, to him who was a protector and not a destroyer. If you were truly Christian, the cross should put you on guard against the kind of enemy with whom you are dealing and teach you the kind of victory to which you should aspire. You carry the symbol of salvation while arranging the death of your brother, and you destroy under the sign of the cross him who was saved by it.

What should I say of these Holy Sacraments which should be the object of the adoration of all Christians and which are the most potent symbol of love and union — what should I say of those Holy Sacraments which are dragged onto the battlefield and in whose presence soldiers, drawn up in battle line, rush forward, brother thrusting his sword into the breast of his brother, while the Christ is made the spectator of these infamous crimes — if indeed Jesus deigns to watch? But the height of absurdity is to see the same sign of the cross shine in both camps, and the same mass said in both camps.

Is there anything more monstrous?[17] How can the cross fight the cross? Can Christ fight Christ? The cross is destined to fill with awe the ranks of the enemies of Christianity. How can Christians fight against what they worship?

I ask you: how can a soldier pray at mass: "Our Father which art in heaven . . ." Oh, sacrilege! How dare you call upon the Father, the common Father, when you prepare to cut the throat of your brother? ". . . Hallowed be Thy Name . . ." But could the name of God be more profaned than by such monstrous deeds and by the hatred that war arouses among men? ". . . Thy kingdom come . . ." How can you ask that, you who have the cruelty to drench the land with the blood of your fellow man? ". . . Thy will be done on earth as it is in Heaven . . ." But his will is that the world should live in peace, and you do nothing but prepare for war! You ask God, who is the common Father of all, for your daily bread, and you burn down the field and the harvest of your brother! And so long as your brothers cannot enjoy the fruit of their labor, you will go so far as to prefer being deprived of it yourself! In spite of all that you dare to add, you who pursue with such fury the destruction of your brother: "And forgive us our trespasses as we forgive those who trespass against us." You try to escape by your prayers the danger of temptation, and you lead your brother into temptation at the risk of your own life. You ask that you be delivered from evil, and yet, guided by evil, you plot the worst evils for your brother.

IV

Plato did not want the struggles which the Hellenes carried on among themselves to be called by the name of war.[18] He did not want to see anything in it but disorder which he called *sedition*. And yet we call war, and even just war, that which Christians wage on Christians, for the most absurd causes and by means of such soldiers and such weapons. Pagan laws require that the one who has dipped his sword in the blood of his brother shall be thrown in the river, sewn in a sack. Are those whom Jesus united by so many bonds less brothers than those united by blood relationship? And yet war rewards parricide. Oh, miserable fate of soldiers! He who is victorious is a parricide. But the vanquished who perished is no less a murderer for having practised murder.

And after all that, we execrate the Turks because they are impious and hostile to the doctrine of Christ, as though the Christians who behave in this way were Christians; or as though there were some spectacle that might be more agreeable to the Turks than to see Christians exterminate each other.

It is said that the Turks make sacrifices to the demons. But is there any spectacle that could be more agreeable to the demons than that of a Christian immolating his fellow-Christian? Then how does the sacrifice of Christians differ from that of the Turks? Besides, the evil spirits rejoice only over a double victim, and is not a double sacrifice what the Christians offer them? Let him who wishes to please the enemies of our faith or be agreeable to demons offer frequent sacrifices of this kind.

But I already hear the excuses alleged by men, so ingenious when it is a question of doing evil to one another. They complain of being forced, in spite of themselves, into war.

Let that mask be stripped from them! Let us deny this false pretext! Let the prince consult his conscience; he will see that it is intolerance or anger, ambition and stupidity, and never necessity, which lead him into war — unless he measures necessity by the ends he pursues, when events do not go according to his views. Let the princes reserve for their own simple people the deceptive tinsel — it is not God whom they will succeed in dazzling by the false sparkle. However, public prayers are uttered everywhere, solemn ceremonies are celebrated, peace is demanded with loud outcries, horrible groans are uttered. "God, give us peace; we implore you to grant our prayers." Could not God rightly reply: "You ask me to deliver you from the evil of which you are yourselves the deliberate authors."

Indeed, if the slightest offense suffices to provoke war, who is the prince who does not ultimately find a pretext? There often occur, between husband and wife, certain incidents to which they must shut their eyes if they do not want affection and friendship to be destroyed. If an incident of this importance arises between princes, must they immediately have recourse to arms? There are laws, there are minds remarkable for their learning, there are besides a great number of abbots and venerable bishops whose advice and intervention might help us avoid the calamities of war. Why do we not prefer to call on such arbitration? However unjust it might be, it could not fail to result in an end less horrible than open war. *There is no peace, even unjust, which is not preferable to the most just of wars.*

If, before making war, a prince examined each thing separately — the expenses the war requires, the advantages that it brings — he would at once realize the benefit he could draw from it.

The consideration which the pontiffs of Rome enjoy is immense. But when one sees nations and their princes grappling with one another and dedicating themselves to truce-

less battle in such cruel wars as have been the case for several
years, one is inclined to ask: Where is the authority of the
popes? What is the power of those who are the highest vicars
of Christ? This is where it should be revealed, if the popes
themselves were not stirred by the same passions. As soon as
a pope calls them to war, everyone hurries to respond. But
let him call them to peace and no one would hasten to obey.
If the princes love peace, as they say, why were they completely submissive to Pope Julius, the instigator of war?
On the other hand, one rarely sees a prince submit to Pope
Leo, who urges harmony and peace.

If the authority of the pontiff of Rome is really inviolable,
should it not make itself felt by urging men to respect peace,
that peace which Jesus especially taught to his disciples? And
do not those princes whom Pope Julius II stirred up to wage
so disastrous a war, when Pope Leo, the most venerated
of pontiffs, was unable to wield the slightest influence over
them in spite of his ardent pacifist exhortations, betray, in
a striking manner, by their attitude the sad truth that under
cover of devotion to the Church they served only their own
base passions? I refrain from saying more.

If they sincerely hated war, I would give some advice by
which they might protect peace. Lasting peace resides not
in the fact of extending, by the aid of marriages, the ties
of relationship among princes, nor in the treaties they draw
up which usually lead to wars. It is necessary to clean out
the very source from which the evil comes, that is, the
absurd and accursed passions which bring about these horrible disorders. For, while each prince satisfies his passions,
the *res publica,* the people's cause, suffers without achieving
what the princes claimed to be seeking at the cost of such base
methods. Let princes use their wisdom to serve not their
passions but their people. Let them be wise so that their
majesty, their wealth, and their magnificence may be measured by what makes them truly great and powerful. Let

them be to their people what a father is to his family. Let a prince consider himself happy only to the extent that he makes his subjects happy. He can be a truly great prince only on condition that he commands free men. He can be truly rich only if he governs a rich people. He is really powerful only if his cities flourish in the midst of perpetual peace.

And that is not all: the nobles and the magistrates must also be in the same frame of mind as their princes; they must weigh everything by the welfare of the state and the nation. That is the only efficacious way of watching over their own interests. Can a king, maintaining this state of mind, ever decide with a light heart to extort money from his people to pay his armies? Would it be admissible for him to reduce his subjects to famine to enrich the leader of an army? Would he expose his subjects to so many perils? I do not believe it.

That is the way a prince should govern his nation so that he may say to himself that, being a man, he commands men; that being free, he commands free men; that being Christian, he commands Christians. For their part, the people must supply him with such means as are necessary to serve the public need. A good prince does not ask more. As for the evil prince, sooner or later the unanimous decision of the people will be able to moderate his passions. In short, on either side, public interest must outweigh private interest.[19]

Let the greatest honors be granted to those among the leaders of the state who, because of their ability and the measures that they have taken, prevent war and establish peace in the world. Let these honors be rendered particularly to those who use all their strength, not to amass the greatest number of soldiers and machines of war, but to seek a way of getting along without them. This praiseworthy precaution has been taken by only one among so many emperors: Diocletian. If he was unable to prevent war, at least he so conducted it that the greatest evils fell on the heads of those who had provoked it.[20] In our time, we see princes make war with absolute impunity, and generals enrich themselves, while all the evils fall on those who work the earth, and on the masses of the people who have no concern in the war and who have encouraged it in no way. What is the wisdom of a prince worth if he does not give to such matters the attention he owes them? What are his feelings worth if he believes these things to be of little importance?

It is indispensable to find some means of preventing the sovereignty of a country from passing so often from hand to hand, as though it moved from one state to another. For novelties in international politics contribute only toward creating trouble, and trouble engenders war. This prevention would become easily possible if young princes took wives from within their own state or, if not, agreed that any prince taking a wife from a neighboring country would lose his rights to the succession of the throne of the said state. Also, a prince should not be permitted to sell or alienate a portion of his domains as though they were private property. Free cities are not private domains, for those where a true king governs are free. Only those commanded by a despot are slaves. Today it may happen that, as a result of marriages, a man born in Ireland becomes king of the Hindus, and another, formerly ruler of Syria, suddenly becomes king of Italy. As a result, neither of the states has a monarch; for, while such a king abandons his first state, the second refuses to recognize him. Its inhabitants declare that he is as unknown to them as though he came from another world. And while he devotes himself to triumphing over the resistance which is raised against him, or in consolidating his authority in his second kingdom, he exhausts and loses the first. Sometimes, he loses both by attempting to govern two states, although he is barely capable of administering one.

Let princes fix once and for all the limits of their states.

These frontiers once established, let no family alliance move them forward or push them back, let no treaty destroy them. Thus, each prince will work to make his country as flourishing as possible. He will devote all his efforts to this one duty so as to leave his children a rich and prosperous country, with the result that this reasonable convention will necessarily contribute to the prosperity of all countries. Besides, princes must not unite among themselves by marriage or by factitious relationships but by sincere and pure friendship and, above all, by the common zeal of deserving well from the human race.

So far as succession to the throne is concerned, the successor of a prince must be the first son by birth or the one whom the vote of the people esteems most capable. As for the other princes, let them resign themselves to be of the rank of the other nobles. *It is a magnificent thing to disregard self-interest and to measure everything by the common interest!*

Finally, it is proper that princes should avoid long voyages, they should never attempt to cross the frontiers of their own countries, recalling always the proverb confirmed by the experience of centuries: "The forehead is nearer than the back of the skull." Let them consider themselves rich not when they despoil their subjects but when they succeed in improving them. When there is a danger of war, let no prince admit to his council young men who dream only of military glory and who do not take account of all the evils that war engenders. Let him keep out, too, those who would profit by the disturbance of the public tranquillity and who would nourish and fatten themselves on the woes of the people. But, on the other hand, let him invite the prudent and the reasonable, whose zeal and love of country are staunch. Finally, he must not undertake a war recklessly with no motive but the caprice of him who desires it, for, once begun, a war is difficult to end.

V

War, which is the most dangerous thing there is, should not be undertaken except with the consent of the entire nation. The causes of war must be suppressed as soon as they manifest themselves. To this end it is necessary to shut our eyes to certain rights; complaisance begets complaisance. *There are cases where we must buy peace.*[21] When one calculates what the war will cost and the number of lives that will be spared by renouncing it, it will seem to be bought very cheaply, whatever one has paid for it. After that, think of all the evils averted and of the goods preserved, and you will not regret what it may have cost.

Meantime, the high ecclesiastical dignitaries must do their duty; the priests must be truly priests, the monks must remember their vows, the theologians must teach what is worthy of Christ — let them understand one another and raise their voices against war! Let them, in public and in private, preach peace, let them glorify and impress it on our souls! If they are powerless to prevent armed conflict, at least let them not approve it, never take part in it, so as not to encourage by their presence the honors awarded for a thing so hateful, or at least so prone to be. It is enough to grant these sacrilegious warriors the tombs they would be refused if they had not fallen in war. If by chance there are honest men among them — and they would constitute only a small number — they would not be cheated of their reward on that account. On the other hand, the impious, who make up the great majority, would be less pleased with themselves if I belittled their merit.

Naturally, I speak of those wars which, for the most futile and unjust causes, generally set Christian against Christian. Certainly, I am not of the same opinion when it is a question of a war in which Christians, aroused by unanimous and pious zeal, repulse the violence of the barbaric invader and protect public tranquillity at the cost of their lives. Unhappily, we see today, exposed in the temples, among the statues of the Apostles and the martyrs, trophies stained with the blood of those for whose salvation Christ shed his own, as though it were more agreeable to God that we make martyrs than become them. It would have sufficed to expose them in public places, or better still, to keep them in some cupboard. It is not suitable to receive in holy temples — which should remain places of immaculate purity — something that is stained with blood. On the other hand, priests, consecrated to God, should never take part in a war except to end it. If they were in agreement and if they made everyone everywhere understand this necessity, the influence of their attitude would be considerable in favor of harmony and peace.

. . . .

Finally, *peace rests largely in the fact of desiring it with all the force of our soul.* Indeed, those who desire it grasp every occasion which is favorable to it. They disregard certain justified claims, smooth over difficulties which oppose it, even endure disagreeable things in order to save that great good which is peace. Unfortunately, it is the opposite that happens. We see today — I will not wear myself out repeating it — princes carefully seeking excuses for war. They suppress and hide everything that might maintain peace; they exaggerate excessively, and to the point of exasperation, everything that would lead to an outbreak of war.

I am ashamed to relate the frightful tragedies caused by lies of this nature, and how *slight and futile are the real causes of the great disasters which afflict humanity.* Influenced by venomous propaganda, everyone then recalls a whole flood of injuries and each one, by exaggerating them, only

increases the evil. While complete forgetfulness of the benefit of peace is being achieved, the slightest hesitation becomes
impossible and all men yearn only for war. That is how it
happens most often that the passions and ambitions of princes
make all the nations in the world take up arms, when public
interest alone, and before all, should be the essential cause of
a war. When these tyrants find nothing that could, even by
grossly exaggerating it, lead to war, they are not troubled
to invent causes to provoke division. They find the means
of dragging other countries into their intrigues without the
slightest reason, setting fire to and fanning among them a
feeling of hatred for each other. That is what the powerful
of this world lend themselves to and watch for, and among
them some priests who fatten on the stupidity and the errors
of the unhappy people by exploiting them for their own
profit.

Thus the Englishman hates the Frenchman for no other
reason than that he is French. The Breton hates the Scot
simply because he is a Scot. The German cannot understand
the Frenchman. The Spaniard disagrees with the German
and with the Frenchman. O cruel human perversity! The
diversity of the vain names they bear is alone sufficient to
divide them to such a point, while the common title of men
and Christians is impotent to unite them! Once more — why
should a thing of so little importance act with more force on
them than all the bonds of nature and Christ? The distance
from one country to another separates bodies and not souls.
Formerly the Rhine separated Frenchmen from Germans; but
the Rhine cannot separate Christian from Christian. The
Pyrenees put a frontier between the Gauls and the Spaniards.
But these same mountains cannot divide human society. The
sea separates the English from the French, but it cannot break
the bonds of the community of Christ.

The Apostle Paul was angry one day when he heard
Christians pronounce these words: "I am Apolinian; I am

Cephean; I am Paulician." He would not permit denominations of this kind that might have wounded Christ, the conciliator of all things. Why do we consider this unlikeness of names, common to each country, as a sufficient reason for nations to destroy one another and tear one another to pieces? Naturally, such a motive cannot absolve those who are lovers of war. So they seek for causes for division and, once they have found them, they rush to divide France. They divide by force this country which neither seas nor mountains nor the various names of its provinces can divide. They make Germans of Frenchmen so that the conformity of the name Frenchman should not preserve union and friendship.

There are disagreeable judicial suits: for example, those for divorce in which the judge does not readily consent to give his judgment and does not admit every testimony. Why should the princes, in as painful and hateful an affair as war, content themselves with the most frivolous reasons?

If name of country is of such a nature as to create bonds between those who have a common country, why do not men resolve that the universe should become the country of all? If blood relationships make those who have the same ancestors friends, is not the Church a great common family to all Christians? If the same house unites the interests of those who live in it, is not the Church the house of all of us? You forgive certain wrongs from your father-in-law simply for the reason that he is your father-in-law, and you will not tolerate anything from him who, by the community of Christian ideals, is your brother? You easily forgive your near relation, and you pardon nothing to him who is your brother in God? What bond should join us more powerfully than the love of Christ? Why pay attention only to what irritates and embitters the soul? Yes, why? If you love peace, say when someone strikes you: "He hurt me, but on other occasions he was good to me, and perhaps he acted on some strange impulse."

Why do men make such great use of their intelligence to harm themselves rather than using all their wisdom to preserve their happiness? Why are they more eager for evil than for good? Those who are even mildly reasonable ordinarily weigh an affair and examine it attentively before deciding. They consider it from all angles and from all points of view. But where war is concerned, men are so hurried that they rush toward their own unhappiness without saying that a war, once unleashed, cannot be checked. Let anyone tell me what war, even the shortest, has not given place to a new war that was infinitely longer? Which is the one that, coming after a longer or shorter peace, has not given place, in repercussions like an echo, to other conflicts? Which, at last, is the one that, not cruel in the beginning, has not become a monstrously bloody war when this evil, by being prolonged, ended by exhausting the nerves of the people to the point of exasperation? If the people are apt to judge but vaguely the gravity of a certain situation, it is up to the princes and their advisers to think for them. It is the duty of the priests to undeceive the people by making them understand by every imaginable argument the error of which they are the victim, and impose their opinion on all by the firmness of their attitude — on those who wish to hear them as well as on those who do not. By making their voices heard everywhere, they will necessarily end by impressing people and making them listen.[22]

Do you want to start a war? Begin by thinking seriously what it may be and what peace is; on the advantages and the disadvantages that each of them brings in its train. Then think long whether it is for the public good that you exchange peace for war. If there is anything really great, it is to see a country living in abundance, flourishing in all the arts, with cities solidly built and well-cultivated fields, enjoying liberal and just laws, cultivating useful sciences, and having irreproachable habits. And now, look in your hearts, princes, and think. If you have ever seen ruined cities, villages reduced to ashes, burned churches, devastated fields, and if this spectacle seems to you as desolate as it is in reality, tell yourself that that is the work of war. If you regard as painful this necessity of bringing into your kingdoms the immense and accursed flood of mercenary soldiers, nourishing them to the ruin of your subjects, seeking to please them, even flattering them — more, confiding yourself and your security to their caprice — tell yourselves once more, O princes, that this evil is the work of war.

If you have a horror of brigandage, what is war but brigandage on a gigantic scale? If you abominate parricide, it is in war that it is learned. What scruple would prevent a man from killing his fellow when, in time of war, human life becomes so cheap that, for a low price, hundreds of men are killed?

War is the scourge of states, the tomb of justice. When the world is at arms, laws are reduced to silence. War encourages murder, opprobrium, adultery, incest. If impiety and forgetfulness of religion are causes of all evils, these two woes are brought to the last extremity by the cruelty of war.[23] A state, we know, disintegrates when the evil have too much authority. In time of war, the evil reign as masters, and those who in times of peace would be put to death become the authors of the most remarkable exploits. Who leads troops most ably along the most tortuous roads if not the brigand so well trained in brigandage? Who sacks private houses and despoils churches with the most courage and coolness if not the sacrilegious and the impious expert in the art of stealing and housebreaking? Who attacks the enemy hardest and exterminates him with the most address if not the professional gladiator or the parricide? Who is the best at burning cities and causing widespread death by using infernal machines of war if not the incendiary? Who has the most contempt for the waves of the ocean and the dangers of the tempest if not the pirate who sails the seas and is trained in murder and pillage?

After that, do you want more evident proofs to show you how infamous war is? Consider by whom it is waged. If it is true that nothing should be dearer to a prince than the well-being of his subjects, there is nothing that he should hate as much as war. If his happiness consists in the fact of commanding a happy people, he ought to cherish peace above all. If a prince should desire primarily to command the best men, it follows that he must have a horror of war and say to himself that it is the source from which spring all iniquities. If he thinks that the more prosperous his people are the more wealth he will possess, he must avoid war by all possible means. However fortunate may be the result of a war, it generally diminishes the wealth of the citizens; and it requires, too, that the army of brigands who wage it be paid with money saved by the people at the cost of so much labor and so much honest effort. Never overlook how vainly princes abandon themselves to illusions as to the causes of war, and about wars themselves which they claim to be just. They let themselves be lulled, without any basis, by the hope of a happy outcome, although this foolish hope is most often exposed by the horrible result of their warlike enterprises.

But let us suppose a cause of war to be perfectly just and its outcome as happy as possible. Then let us calculate all the disadvantages and all the advantages resulting from victory. The final conclusion would be, in any case, that *there is no victory which does not do evil to men, for there is none which is not stained with human blood.* Let us add to this sorrow the relaxation of manners and of discipline in the people — evils which can scarcely be remedied. But that is not all. Even victory cannot be obtained by the prince save by exhausting the public treasury, by despoiling the people, by crushing the good, by encouraging the wicked to crime. And when the victorious war is over, there is general decay which will long be felt.

Meanwhile arts perish and commerce languishes. A prince cannot block the enemy at his frontiers without being forced at the same time to isolate his own country from many other states. O prince! Before the war, all the neighboring countries belonged to you, for *peace, by means of commercial exchange, makes all things common.* Now examine the frightful consequences of your bellicose action: in time of war you are scarcely the master of your own country!

To destroy a city, how many machines of war you need, how many tents to lodge your army. You have to improvise a semblance of a city in order to wipe out a real one. With far less expense you could have built a new city. To prevent the enemy from leaving his fortress, you exile yourself from your own country, you sleep on the hard ground. *It would have cost far less to build new cities than to demolish with your war machines existing cities.* However vast they may be, I am not going to calculate here the sums of money that run through the hands of the furnishers of armies and other profiteers of war, as well as through the hands of generals. But if you yourself make an exact calculation of the whole of this waste, and if, after that, you do not admit that you could have with a tenth part bought peace, I will accept with resignation being driven off.

You will reply, I know, that it is wrong for an elevated spirit not to avenge himself for injuries. No! There is no more certain indication of a debased soul — particularly for a king — than the fact of avenging himself. Your Majesty thinks he is lacking in his honorable duty when, having dealings with a neighboring prince, perhaps your relation or ally, having perhaps even done him some services and having deserved his gratitude, you yield the smallest of your rights. But how much more do you humiliate yourself when, abandoned to the discretion of your soldiers — this execrable band of insatiable criminals — you are constantly forced to appease them with gold; or when you send ambassadors to hire the treacherous and cruel Carians,[24] and confide your own person and the fate of your family to these faithless and lawless brutes.

In the case where it would seem to a prince that a bought peace would bring with it some injustice, let him not say, "I lose this sum," but rather let him say, "I am buying peace cheap." In such a situation, any wise prince should declare, "If the affair concerned me alone, I would refrain from such a purchase. But I am a prince, and, whether I like it or not, I must keep in sight the interests of my people."

The prince whose sole goal is the public welfare does not easily start a war. Unfortunately, in our time we see that almost all the causes of war spring from motives that have nothing to do with the common good. You want to get back some territory, but how does this return of territory concern your people? You want to avenge yourself on him who abandoned your daughter? That has nothing to do with the state! It is the duty of princes and of wise men to meditate on these questions and to solve them.

What prince has ever ruled more magnificently and over a greater people than the Emperor Octavius Augustus? Well, this great prince would willingly even have renounced his power if he had found another prince whose wisdom was better for the state than his own. It is with justification that remarkable authors have so praised the famous words of this illustrious emperor: "May my sons go if another prince be more capable than they to make himself useful to the state." It was pagans who professed sentiments of this nature, so in harmony with the Christian doctrine. And Christian princes despise Christian people to such a point that they are ready to avenge their personal injuries and assuage their passions at the price of a world cataclysm! And after all these statements, there are still hypocritical princes who claim loudly that they cannot feel safe except by destroying the multitude of evil men!

Why, among so many Roman emperors, were only the two Antonines not attacked — one called the *pious,* the other the *philosopher?* Is it not because no prince rules in greater security than he who is always willing to abandon his place — that is, he who rules not for his own advantage but for the good of the state?

If, therefore, nothing can move you, neither feeling for humanity nor respect owed to religion, nor so many miseries and calamities, at least let the *dignity* of the Christian name, which you cover with shame, bring back your souls to harmony. How small a part of the world is occupied by Christians! And yet this is the Eternal City, situated on a high mountain, destined to serve as a spectacle to God and to the world. Imagine what the enemies of the Christian world must think and say of us, the opprobrium that they throw on Christ, when they see his disciples destroy one another for more frivolous causes than those of the pagans, more cruel than those of the impious, and, by means of machines, more inhuman than theirs.

For who invented cannons? Was it not Christians? And that the indignity of this thing may be still more revolting, the field cannons are given the name of the Apostles, are painted with images representing the saints. O cruel irony! Would Paul, that great apostle, who always preached peace, have directed against Christians such infernal machines?

If we want to convert the non-Christians to Christianity, it is indispensable that we first be Christian ourselves. They will never believe us to be so as long as they see that the evil which Jesus so detested is sown nowhere in the world with more violence than by the Christians. Homer was surprised that the pagans, in spite of all the charm and the delight that they experienced from certain pleasures — of which the most appreciated were eating and drinking, dancing and hearing music — always ended by becoming tired of them, while they were never tired of waging war, however disastrous it might be. This astonishment of Homer's is far more justified in relation to Christians, to whom not only the monstrousness of war itself but the very word *war* should inspire horror.

Warlike as was ancient Rome, one yet saw the temple of Janus closed from time to time.[25] That proves that there were periods in which the Romans enjoyed peace. Is there anyone who can say as much of Christian peoples? One sees among them no truce of arms; they are always fighting each other. How, under these conditions, do Christians have the temerity to preach the doctrine of Christ to the worshipers of Mohammed? Nothing, on the contrary, could arouse more courage in the Turks than the division that reigns among the Christians, for there is nothing easier to conquer than those who are divided. Therefore, Christians, do you want to make the Turks afraid? Agree among yourselves!

VI

Why do you reject for yourselves and your generation the happiness of life? Why do you want to alienate yourself from future felicity? Is the life of men not already subject to enough misery? Harmony greatly softens miseries and misfortunes of men. As long as they are united, as long as they help one another and are good to each other, they find consolation. So long as soul can communicate with soul and good will reigns among them, all the happiness which is imparted to them only makes this union sweeter and closer.

Remember that there is nothing more frivolous or less durable than the pretended causes that hurl men into battle against each other. Death spares no one; it threatens the powerful as well as common men. Yes, how great are those storms unleashed by man, this minute animal who vanishes like smoke! At the end of this short life is eternity. Yet we exhaust ourselves by pursuing quite illusory advantages as though this life would last eternally. O unhappy ones, who do not believe or aspire to the happiness of the just! O imprudent ones, who believe you can attain happiness by war! For what is happiness? Is it anything but the effect of the understanding between fortunate souls who, at the same time, achieve perfectly among themselves what Jesus with all his strength demanded of the Heavenly Father, when he begged him to unite his disciples as strongly as he and his Father are united? How can you expect ever to be ready for this supreme harmony if you do not force yourselves to achieve this harmony here below? Just as a contemptible gormandizer could not transform himself suddenly into an angel, so a bloody soldier could not become a companion of the martyrs.

It is time to amend your ways. If the shedding of *Christian* blood seems to you of little importance, then more than enough *human* blood has flowed so that this frenzy of exterminating each other should come to an end. You have sacrificed enough to the infernal furies. You have offered enough spectacles to delight the Turks. Fix your attention on the miseries endured by humanity during and after any war. Let us put to the account of destiny all the follies that have been committed up to now; and let Christians, as some noble pagans of ancient times tried with success, approve and practice forgetfulness of past injuries. Then apply yourselves by common consultations and deliberations to achieving peace. Use all your strength to establish this peace, not with weak threads but on solid and indestructible foundations.

I call on you, Princes, whose will principally shapes the position of the people and who should represent among men the image of Christ. Hear the voice of our Lord and Master which exhorts you to peace. Say to yourselves that all humanity, stifling under the burden of evil which has crushed it for so long, implores you ardently. Let those who feel themselves limited in their rights, and who feel sorrow at not being able to wage war any longer, preach peace for the happiness of all. This enterprise is too important for slight arguments to hold back its realization.

I call on you, Priests, who are consecrated to God, to preach with all the strength of your soul what you know to be most agreeable to our Father, to fight what he held most in horror.

I call on you, Theologians; preach the Gospel of peace, make it ring ceaselessly in the ears of the people.

I call on you, Bishops, high dignitaries of the Church: let your authority have enough influence to establish peace on indestructible foundations.

I call on you, Magistrates and Powerful Ones of the earth, who occupy the highest rank in the states, that you aid with all your ability the wisdom of the princes and the vicars of Christ.

I call at last on all those who pride themselves in the title of Christians, that they conspire, together and with all their strength, against war! That in each state they show the weight of the union of all against the tyranny of the powerful. That each one contribute all that he has with a view to establishing peace. That eternal harmony may unite those whom nature and Christ have already united by so many bonds. That the effort of each strive toward the realization of what will contribute to the happiness of all.

Everything invites us to it. First, the sense of nature and, in a way, humanity itself. Next, Christ, prince and author of all human felicity. Finally, all the advantages of peace and all the horrors of war. Let the soul of princes, animated by divine inspiration, aspire to peace and invoke it. But I see the pacific and gentle Leo wave in the air the sign of peace, inviting, like a real vicar of Christ, the whole world to harmony.[26] If you are his sheep, follow your shepherd. If you are his children, follow your father. The most Christian of princes, King Francis I, he who did not hesitate to buy peace and never made an issue of his Majesty, worked for peace in every imaginable way, teaching the world that *the most sublime thing is to deserve well of the human race.* The most illustrious of princes, Charles of Austria, a young man of irreproachable character, desires it. Emperor Maximilian does not despise it. King Henry VIII of England does not disparage it. It is proper that we imitate the example of so many good princes.

Most of the people detest war and desire peace. A small number, whose accursed happiness always depends upon the misfortune of the common people, want war. Must their inhumanity outweigh the will of so many good people? Look to the past and see that up to now nothing has been definitely established, either by treaties or by family alliances, by force or by vengeance; nothing guarantees against danger so surely as kindness and good will. Wars lead to wars. Vengeance attracts vengeance. Indulgence creates indulgence. Good will invites to good will. Thus those who yield even a small part of their rights will enjoy the greatest consideration.

The result of men's efforts has not always been the realization of the desired object. But God prospers with his wise advice the enterprises conducted under his auspices and in the spirit of Christ. He will protect and support those who favor peace, who sacrifice the most to public interest, knowing that, while sacrificing it to the happiness of all, they contribute to the assurance of their own happiness.

The princes will truly reign with majesty when they command happy and virtuous people, so as to rule by laws rather than by arms. Nobles will have more worthy nobility. Priests will spend more calmly the moments which they devote to their meditations. The people will benefit with more peaceful tranquillity, with greater abundance, in security. The name of Christian will become more imposing to the enemies of the cross. All those who belong to the human race will assist one another, thus making themselves dear to Christ, to him who always loved the highest happiness.

THUS SPOKE PEACE

Translator's Notes

1. Philip of Burgundy, Bishop of Utrecht, youngest brother of David, who had preceded him in the same bishopric and who had ordained Erasmus priest (in 1492). Philip was the youngest and David the oldest of the many natural sons of Philip the Good, the mightiest and most famous among the dukes of Burgundy. Thus, by his father, Philip the bishop was a half-brother of Charles the Bold, too, the heir to the throne of that dukedom and father-in-law of Maximilian I. Nine years after the death of his father and in spite of his illegitimacy, Philip was brought to court. He was then twelve. Six years later he became one of the commanders of Maximilian and soon afterwards coadjutor to his brother David. At the age of thirty-six he was named admiral of Flanders, and the next year he accompanied Philip the Fair, his half-grandnephew, to Spain. It was on the return of the latter that Erasmus delivered his *Panegyric* in the ducal palace at Brussels. (Philip the Fair was the father of Charles V.) At the age of forty-four, Philip was in Rome as ambassador of Maximilian to the Holy See. He returned home profoundly disgusted by the immorality which he witnessed at the papal court. In March 1517, when he was fifty-three years old, he was elected Bishop of Utrecht, succeeding thus to the see of his brother, who had died in 1496. The year of Philip's accession to the Bishopric of Utrecht coincided with that of the publication of *Peace Protests!*

   By his various titles, his connections, his wealth, and his personal qualities as well, Philip was, at the time when Erasmus made public his peace manifesto, one of the most influential personalities in Christendom. Erasmus met him on various occasions. Knowing how horrified Philip was by the morals of the highest clergy in the capital of the Christian world, Erasmus believed in his sincerity and hoped — in vain! — to make of him a powerful ally in his struggle for universal peace. Hence this dedication (lacking in the translation of *Querela Pacis* by Thomas Paynell).

2. In the *Odyssey* Homer tells of a sorceress, Circe, daughter of Helios, the god of the sun. She dwelt on the island of Aeaea where she first feasted those who came there, and then by magic transformed them into beasts. Odysseus set out to release some of his companions who had been thus transformed. He was provided by Hermes with the herb moly, which prevented him from succumbing to Circe's spells. (See Webster's *New International Dictionary*.)

3. Erasmus here formulates the principle of the origin of human society, but without developing it, because it seemed so indisputable to him. Others did so later, particularly Jean-Jacques Rousseau, who, toward the middle

185

of the eighteenth century, brilliantly developed this idea in his *Discourse on the Origin of Inequality*.

4. The few examples here only hint at Erasmus' vivid interest in nature. This great observer of life and men liked to illustrate and emphasize his points and his ideas by analogies drawn from nature. Flowers, trees, wild and domestic animals, snakes, fish, birds, stones, metals, rivers, winds, stars — he spoke of them like an intimate friend (though — oddly enough for a painter and friend of painters — Erasmus never described or mentioned a landscape or any vast panorama of nature). In other works, he pointed out at length, not only the affinities which invite to peace but the repulsion that men and things instinctively feel for one another. Nonetheless, even from this disagreement and repulsion he could draw useful lessons, principles to make our life, if not happy, at least less unhappy than it often is through our own fault.

Erasmus collected a considerable number of these principles in *Colloquies*, his longest work. In these lively dialogues, which sparkle with humor and irony, some of which have justly been compared with those of Socrates, the wisdom of Erasmus, fruit of a lifetime of nearly seventy years, is unfolded with fascinating richness. While in *Peace Protests!* he draws upon nature to make clear the essence of peace, he makes use of it in one of his dialogues to draw a fine distinction between real friendship, which depends on natural affinities, and charitable love for men in general, in accordance with the teachings of religion. It is still peace — with oneself and with others — which concerns him.

After an extended excursion into the vegetable, mineral, and animal realms and the elements, of which he shows more than a hundred remarkable specimens, Erasmus pauses to confront nature itself with man's nature and draws for his young companion the following conclusion:

"There are men who expect their happiness from necromancy, others from the stars. I believe that one can find no more certain felicity than in abstaining from every kind of life for which one instinctively feels a secret horror, and in embracing the mode of existence for which one feels an inclination, with the exception, of course, of evil. One must also withdraw from the company of those whose character does not suit one's own, and attach oneself only to those toward whom one is drawn by an instinctive affinity."

"If that were done, friends would be rare," the young man objected.

"Obviously," Erasmus explained, "charity extends to all, but friendship must be reserved for a few. And he who wrongs none of his fellow men, however evil they may be, and rejoices even if they become better, loves all the human race, in my opinion, sufficiently like a Christian." (*Colloquies*, "On Friendship.")

5. According to Erasmus, all unusurped power, whether dynastic or otherwise, rests on a democratic, electoral principle: the will of the people. On close study of this question, one sees that the founders of the ruling dynasties were indeed originally elected by the people to administer public affairs, because of their particular gifts and their superior virtues. On election, they assumed obligations toward those who entrusted them with the burden of governing them. The descendants of these chosen men

should, therefore, consider themselves as bound by the same obligations; and the people have a right to expel them if they violate the agreement that determined the choice of their first predecessor. This idea of the democratic origin of kingship had already been touched on by Aristotle and taken up timidly by certain authors before Erasmus — especially by Dante in *De Monarchia,* in disagreement on this point with Thomas Aquinas. Trusting that divine justice would control the acts of princes, Thomas Aquinas would not accept the right of the people to oppose their sovereigns, epecially to resist them by violence.

Erasmus returns to this important question more than once. Particularly in *Institutio Principis Christiani,* he specifies plainly and courageously, not only the obligations of the prince but the rights of the people. One will read farther on in *Peace Protests!* the discreet but frank passage in which he sets the princes on guard against a legitimate uprising of the people, to rid themselves of rulers who violate their obligations.

After Erasmus, this question was brought more and more into prominence — first by Thomas More in *Utopia* — and it has not been dropped since. Fénelon, Hobbes, and Locke are its most illustrious exponents. But it was Jean-Jacques Rousseau who stated it most clearly in his *Social Contract.* People were soon to abandon theory and put this fertile idea into practice in the American Revolution, the French Revolution, the nineteenth century, and our own. Erasmus' idea has proved to be a long-range shot.

6. The interminable disputes of the scholastics and the subjects of these disputes were favorite targets of Erasmus. Against them he directed his sarcasm and his most biting irony, particularly against the schools with Thomas Aquinas and Scotus ("who bristles more than a hedgehog") at their head. He accused them of having distorted the doctrine of Jesus and of having buried it under the impenetrable accumulation of their casuistic reasoning, which was more dangerous than useless. Useless, because the doctrine of Jesus is so simple that it requires no commentary and is sufficient unto itself. Dangerous, because they make religion insipid and, by obscuring it and imposing their opinions like dogmas, they create skeptics and propagate irreligion. Besides, they prevent the reading of Holy Scripture. According to Erasmus, Christianity is a moral system and a practical philosophy rather than an irrational belief. In speaking of the doctrine of Jesus, Erasmus often referred to it as "Philosophia Christi." The scholastic theologians poisoned this pure spring as much by their ignorance and cruel intolerance as by their vice of self-exaggeration.

It is in *Enchiridion Militis Christiani,* which appeared in 1504 and which, for all its brevity, probably remains his keenest exposé of the evangelical doctrine, that Erasmus declared war on scholasticism. He continued the attack in his succeeding works and in his rich correspondence. But it was in *Praise of Folly* that he ridiculed scholasticism most effectively.

7. Although Erasmus was himself a monk, no author, not even Voltaire, has expressed more contempt for monks of all orders or has ridiculed

them with sharper darts. What he says of them in *Peace Protests!* is only
a pale reflection of what he said elsewhere. Here, as an illustration, is
a famous passage from *Praise of Folly:*

"Here are some other people whom I [Folly] make almost as happy as
the theologians. They are those who are usually called men of religion,
or monks, although these two names do not suit them at all, as there is
perhaps no one who has less religion than the majority of these men of
religion, and one encounters these so-called monks or recluses everywhere.
. . . Convinced that the greatest piety consists of the most squalid ignorance, they make it a point of glory to be unable to read. When, in
their churches, they bray with a stupid air the psalms they do not
understand, they are persuaded that God, the angels, and all the saints
of paradise take great pleasure in hearing them. There are among them
those who, proud of their filth and their want, go from door to door,
demanding charity with extreme arrogance and effrontery. At inns, in
carriages, by land, by sea, one meets them everywhere. Everywhere
they besiege you and extort by their insistence charity of which they
deprive the real poor. Such are the illustrious personages who, with their
dirt, their ignorance, their coarseness and their impudence, claim to re-
trace the life of the apostles.

"Is there anything more distorted than all those minute practices
which regulate all their actions with a kind of mathematical exactitude,
and whose slightest violation is a crime that must be expiated? The
number of knots that fasten their shoes, the color and length of the belt,
the cut of their robe, the material of which it is made, the shape and
precise size of the cowl, the exact diameter of the tonsure, the number
of hours devoted to sleep — everything is determined, measured, fixed.
Judge of the fine effect that this uniformity must produce on minds and
bodies that differ so among themselves!

"And yet it is because of all these imbecilities that they make light
of the laymen and that they have the greatest contempt for one another.
A belt that is a little different, a habit of a deeper or lighter shade —
nothing more is necessary to start the bloodiest quarrels among people
who profess to exercise the charity of the apostles. Some of them carry
the spirit of penitence to the point of wearing habits of the commonest
and coarsest material, but next to their skin they wear the finest shirts.
Others, on the contrary, wear the shirts outside and the woolen garments
underneath. We see those who shiver at the sight of money and those
who would rather touch a poisonous snake than the smallest coin, but
these good fathers are not so scrupulous when it comes to wine or girls.

"With what care each group of monks tries to distinguish itself from the
others! Their greatest desire is not to resemble Jesus Christ but not to
resemble one another. Thus they derive much of their happiness from
the surnames they have given themselves. Some are proud to be called
Franciscans, and these Franciscans are divided into Recollets, Minorites,
Minims, Bullists. Then come the Benedictines, the Bernardines, the Brigit-
tains, the Augustines, the Guillelmites, the Jacobins. And they take
pride in all these names as though it were too little to be called simply
Christians.

"Most of these people have so much confidence in their ceremonies and their little human traditions that they are convinced that paradise is not too great a recompense for a life spent in the observation of all these fine things. They do not think that Jesus Christ, despising all these vain practices, will ask them whether they observed the great precept of charity on which is founded the whole law that he gave to men. . . . But Jesus Christ, at last interrupting this inexhaustible flow of their boasting, will say:

" 'What is this new type of Pharisee? I gave only one law to men, it is the only one that I recognize, and the only one of which these people do not speak. It is not for robes, prayers, abstinences, continual fasts, that I formerly promised my Father's kingdom, but for the practice of all the duties of charity — and I explained myself then *clearly and without parable*. I do not know these people who are aware so well of the merit of their good works, and who wish to appear more holy than I. Let them seek another paradise than mine, let them demand one of those [i.e. the saints or founders of the monastic orders] whose vain and absurd traditions they have followed in preference to my doctrine!'

"When they hear this sentence and see that, in paradise, charitable sailors and cart drivers are preferred to them, how do you imagine they will look?"

8. Eris — Goddess of Discord. It was she who, at the marriage of Peleus and Thetis to which she was not invited, threw into the assembly of the Greek gods the apple of discord. Hera, Athena, and Aphrodite claimed it, and Zeus referred the decision to Paris of Troy, who awarded it to Aphrodite.

9. This is a theme familiar from earliest antiquity, one that finds its best modern expression in Prince Kropotkin's work, *Mutual Aid*. The reader feels here that Erasmus was an assiduous student of the classics. "Men are born for mutual assistance," we read, for example, in *De Ira* by Seneca.

10. This passage is of basic importance in any history of the Reformation. Here as elsewhere, in his works as in his letters, nothing could make clearer the reasons for the irreconcilable antagonism between Erasmus and Luther than the wholly peaceful and undogmatic concept of religion of the former and the bellicose mission which the German Reformer attributed to it and which he carried out in word and deed.

It is the same with the democratic idea and the right of revolt against the oppressor which the humanist proclaimed, and Luther's totalitarian concept of the unconditional obedience of the people to their masters. For Erasmus, peace and charity were the two columns on which the doctrine of Jesus rested. In politics it was the will of the people and not of the prince that was the basis of all legal government. And the people don't want war, he went on repeating tirelessly, the people don't want tyranny.

The way in which Luther opposed these two concepts of Erasmus and the language which he used in refuting Erasmus are not lacking in savor:

"You [Erasmus] cannot make of the sword a pen, or of war — peace. The word of God means *war*, it means wrath, a swallowing up *(Untergang)*, poison."

To the reiterated appeal of Erasmus for the reform of Rome and the Church, without a destruction of the unity and the universality of the Church lest it become national and sectarian, Luther replied:

"Stop whining and lamenting: there is little medicament against this fever. This war is that of our Lord, it is he who provoked it, and it will not cease until the enemies of his Word are reduced to nothing."

And as Erasmus, with his spirit of tolerance, his prestige, and his literary genius was more dangerous to Luther than all the Pope's bulls and the opponents in Rome, the German Reformer turned all his heavy artillery against the peaceful humanist when he perceived that he could no longer gain the latter's unconditional support:

"He who destroys Erasmus will destroy a bug which will stink worse dead than alive."

With his friends assembled at table, he banged his heavy fist and cried out:

"I will put it in my Testament and I take you all as witnesses that I consider Erasmus the greatest enemy of Christ, greater than all those who have been born in the last thousand years."

As for the right of the people to rise against an oppressor-prince, Luther, although morally responsible for the uprising of the German peasants against the tyranny of the landlords and government, encouraged the princes to crush them pitilessly. This is how he expresses his views on a subject dear to Erasmus:

"He who perishes at the side of his prince will become a happy martyr. He who falls on the other side will go straight to the Devil. That is why it is the duty of everyone who can do so, whether secretly or openly, to strike him down, to cut his throat, to run him through, keeping always in mind that there is nothing more venomous, more noxious, or more diabolical than a rebel." For "the ass needs kicks and the plebeian needs to be governed with violence."

After the savage crushing of the peasant revolt which cost the lives of a hundred thousand poor fellows, with Thomas Münzer at their head — a cruelty which filled Erasmus with horror and disgust — Luther, without the slightest compunction, had the bad taste to boast of his role in that massacre in the following terms:

"I, Martin Luther, cut down the rebellious peasants because it was I who ordered their death. All their blood is on my hands *(all ihr Blut ist auf meinem Hals)* ."

And in his *Table Talk,* we find still another comment in the same taste, made to the friends gathered around him:

"I order you, at the command of God, to be enemies of Erasmus and to be on guard against his books. I will write against him, even if he should die and perish from it; I will kill Satan with my pen, as I killed Thomas Münzer whose blood covers my hands."

Such specimens of Luther's utterances are more revealing than all the works on doctrine that have been devoted for centuries to the reasons that forced Erasmus to dissociate his name from that of Luther, although, before Luther, he had prepared the ground for the reform of the church. But Luther's words have another meaning of far more burning timeliness. For it was Luther who shaped the nationalistic and boastful mentality of the German people. It was Luther who commanded them to renounce all political initiative and to submit to their master or *Führer*. (See, in particular, Luther's *Von weltlicher Obrigkeit, wie weit man ihr Gehorsam schuldig sei*.) When one reads these sanguinary and savage statements (in *Table Talk*), which constitute the family reading of the German Lutherans, can one still be surprised that Germany followed Hitler with the same gaiety of heart that, 450 years ago, it followed, in his violence and hatred, him whom it made the prophet of its national religion?

And is it not significant that the word used by the Nazis, as the vilest insult, against those Germans who, although "Aryans," disagreed with them and their rule, as well as to vilify everything foreign or which did not fit into the Hitlerian "philosophy," was taken from Luther: *undeutsch,* i.e. *un-German?* It is characteristic of Luther's nationalistic conception of his new creed that he coined this word in his translation of the New Testament where he rendered *barbarian* (I Corinthians XIV:11) as *undeutsch*. This fact is generally forgotten, since the Bible Society, in printing its modernized version, has charitably replaced that term with a word adequate to Paul's original. (See, for instance, the 1942 edition of Luther's Bible by the American Bible Society.)

In spite of all these disturbing coincidences, it is nevertheless certain that, could Luther have foreseen them as well as the ungodly Hitlerism in general, they would have filled him with horror. Luther was a profoundly religious and unselfish man with no other purpose than to serve God, to spread and to defend God's truth — but the truth as that violent mystic envisioned it.

11. In *Institutio Principis Christiani*, Erasmus expatiated at length on morality and the meaning of international treaties. See above, page 65.

12. In old Latin literature, these abject personages were often decried and cursed by the great poets, particularly Virgil and Ovid. Dionysius the Ancient was an odious tyrant of Syracuse. Mezentius, King of Agylla in Etruria, was driven out by its inhabitants because of his cruelty. Phalaris, tyrant of Agrigente (Sicily), was massacred by the people in revolt.

13. Erasmus had considerable influence on Voltaire, who paid him the highest tribute in his writings. In the present case, where the pacifist ideas of Erasmus are concerned, it is enough to read the article "Guerre" (*War*) in the *Dictionnaire Philosophique* of Voltaire, to form an idea of this influence on the greatest French writer of the eighteenth century. Voltaire wrote:

"It seems that since God has endowed men with reason, this reason should warn them not to abase themselves by imitating beasts, particularly since nature has given them neither arms for killing their fellow men nor an instinct that leads them to suck their blood."

14. This refers to a verse in Ovid's *Fastes*. The Latin poet's loathing for war was vehemently expressed on several occasions.

15. This refers to a group of cardinals who "distinguished" themselves in the wars undertaken by Pope Julius II, and those who encouraged Louis XII and Emperor Maximilian to call the Council of Pisa followed by the schism. These cardinals took so active a part in the war that Cardinal

Amboise, old and mortally ill, even had himself carried onto the battle-field in a litter in order to encourage the fighters. But the cardinal at whom Erasmus strikes most frequently, without naming him, is Schinner. He was a vile prince of the church and the one most closely heeded by Pope Julius II. It was he who encouraged the Pope, not only to declare war on the Venetians but in all his warlike enterprises. The Pope re-warded him by raising him to the dignity of cardinal.

16. Doubtless this refers to Cardinal Schinner. In order to flatter the Swiss, among whom the pope recruited his mercenaries, Julius II appointed Schinner Legate of War, Schinner himself being Swiss. As Legate of War, he enjoyed the full powers of the Holy See in Lombardy and Ger-many, and was in charge of the war against France. The flag with the cross is doubtless the one that Julius II gave to the Swiss mercenaries in recognition of their services. It was decorated with a cross, and the Swiss fought under this flag. (On this subject see the erudite and stimulating work of A. Büchi: *Kardinal Matthäus Schinner als Staatsmann und Kir-chenfürst.*)

17. Compare with Voltaire's comment in his article on war in the *Diction-naire Philosophique:*
    "The marvelous thing about this infernal enterprise is that each leader of the murderers had his flag blessed and solemnly called upon God be-fore going out to exterminate his neighbor. If a leader had the happiness of slaughtering only two or three thousand men, he did not praise God; but when there were about ten thousand exterminated by fire and steel and, as an extra favor, some city was razed, they sang a long four-part song, composed in an unknown tongue [Latin] and crammed with barbar-isms, for all those who fought. The same song serves for marriages and births as well as for murders, which is unpardonable, especially in the nation most famous for its new tunes.
    "Natural religion has a thousand times prevented citizens from com-mitting crimes. A well-born soul has no will for it; a tender soul, imagin-ing a stern and just God, is afraid of it. But artificial religion encourages all the cruelties that are carried on in company: conspiracies, sedition, brigandage, snares, attacks on cities, pillaging, murder. Each one marches gaily to crime under the banner of his Saint."

18. *The Republic*, Part III.

19. In *Institutio Principis Christiani*, Erasmus draws superb portraits of the Tyrant and the Good Prince, examining them feature by feature:
    "The tyrant administers his state by violence, by trickery and by the most perfidious methods; he has in view only his personal interests. The real king is inspired by wisdom, reason, and beneficence; he thinks only of the welfare of the state. The tyrant does his best to see that the property of his people passes into the hands of a small number of the privileged, who are usually the vilest subjects of his state, in order to build his power on the ruin of his people; whereas the good king thinks that only the wealth of the citizens can assure his own wealth. The former so acts as to keep everything dependent on him by laws and by informers. The good king always takes delight in the freedom of the

citizens. One has, for the protection of his person, guards, mercenaries and brigands; the other thinks that his beneficence toward the citizen and a similar feeling on the part of his subjects will suffice to protect him. The despot takes pleasure in the perfidy with which he provokes factions and cabals. He nourishes and encourages the slightest divisions which are manifested among his subjects in order to exercise more easily his tyranny. The good prince strives to maintain harmony, to calm the slightest dissensions which arise among his subjects, for he knows that the dissension among citizens of the same state is the plague of the nations. And while the despot has recourse to illusory pretexts to unleash war whenever he feels that the state is becoming too flourishing, finding in this way a sure means of exhausting the resources of his subjects, the good king does the impossible and even makes sacrifices to maintain public peace. He wants it to be perpetual, realizing that all the sorrows of a state are engendered by war."

20. In his *Utopia,* Thomas More, through the mouth of Hythlodee, fully develops the idea of the exemplary punishment of the aggressor, in order to discourage in the future those who plan to attack their peaceful neighbors. But, even when victorious, the Utopians were so depressed with their work that their moral sense would have revolted if anyone had seen in the war records of their citizens "courage," "valor," or "heroism," as is done in the nations of our world. One must fight when evil people force one to it, but it is shameful to associate the highest moral qualities with murder, destruction, and devastation. How, this filthy task accomplished, can one celebrate it with holidays and public rejoicing, when one knows what mourning and misfortune such a punitive enterprise leaves behind? Punish the aggressor; but after having left him in no position for destruction, return home, sad and even ashamed, and go back to work, trying to forget as quickly as possible what you were forced to do in self-defense! Among earthly inhabitants, however, commemorative dates are even set on which, year after year, they celebrate joyously the success of their murderous arms, even having their children take part.

21. The idea of "buying peace" will soon be taken up again by François Rabelais, and nearly two centuries later by Fénelon. Since then, this argument has continually been debated by greatest thinkers.

22. See above, pp. 90-91.

23. All those who write against the scourge of war agree that it generates most of the vices, and that all vices taken together fail to equal the monstrousness of war, which exceeds them all. Church sermons are directed against vices, or so-called vices, without, however, always attacking them at their root, which is war. Voltaire, as an inspired disciple of Erasmus, was indignant at the position taken by the preachers as well as at the writings of those moralists and philosophers who laid down rules of life, rules of ethics, and of an exemplary existence, while overlooking the greatest of evils — war! To attack them, Voltaire chose as his target the most popular among them, Louis Bourdaloue.

Bourdaloue was one of the greatest French preachers of the seventeenth century and the famous author of *Sermons*, a masterpiece of French classical literature. Because of his remarkable style and his penetrating analysis of morals, some of his pages still have a surprising freshness. Bourdaloue was a Jesuit and his "Sermon on Impurity," to which Voltaire refers, is reputed to be one of the best delivered by this eminent preacher:

"You have made a very poor sermon on impurity, O Bourdaloue! But none on the many kinds of murder, on rape, on brigandage, on the universal rage which devastate the world. All the vices of all ages and all places would never equal the evils that result from a single campaign.

"Miserable doctors of souls, you cry for an hour and a quarter over pinpricks and you say nothing about the malady that is tearing us into thousand pieces! Moralist philosophers, burn all your books! So long as the caprice of a few men can legally destroy thousands of our brothers, that part of the human race consecrated to heroism will be the most frightful in all nature." (Article "Guerre" [*War*] *in Dictionnaire Philosophique*.)

24. Inhabitants of ancient Caria, a warlike people, now extinct. They were famous for their courage and cruelty. Christian countries of Europe recruited among them mercenaries for their fighting armies.

25. It is doubtful whether Peace, in recalling the occasional closing of the Janus temple in Ancient Rome, is choosing her ground well. What did this temple mean to the Romans and how often was it closed as a sign of reigning peace? A kind of tunnel, improperly called "temple" and situated near the Forum, it was consecrated by King Numa to the good King of Latium, Janus, when the latter, after death, was proclaimed a God and patron of Rome. Whenever the country was at war, the Janus temple remained open as a sign that its divine inhabitant had left at the head of the army. When peace came and the patron of Rome was supposed to have returned, the temple was shut in order to prevent Janus from leaving it. But such occasions presented themselves only three times in seven hundred years! — the first time under Numa, another time after the Second Punic War, and the third time under Emperor Augustus. Thus the reminder by Peace that even in Ancient Rome the Janus temple was "closed" from time to time" is rather an overstatement — unless Peace estimated that in the course of the seven centuries preceding the age of Erasmus, Christendom had not known even three intervals of peace, and that the Roman warriors, when compared with Christian rulers, were still exemplary peace-lovers.

26. With all the respect due to popes, it must be said that Leo X had not lived up to the hopes Erasmus had placed in him. Less warlike than his predecessor Julius II, he was nonetheless a warmonger and a political intrigant, more indeed a politician than a pope, more devoted to letters and arts than to the Church, more eager to defend the interests and to regain much of the lost power of his Medici family than to watch over the heritage of Saint Peter and to maintain peace.

Index